Mafeking Diary

Mafeking Diary

A Black Man's View
of a White Man's War

Sol T. Plaatje

edited by John Comaroff
with
Brian Willan and Andrew Reed

MERIDOR BOOKS CAMBRIDGE
IN ASSOCIATION WITH
JAMES CURREY LONDON
OHIO UNIVERSITY PRESS ATHENS

Published by
Meridor Books
Meridor House, Main Street
Shudy Camps, Cambridge CB1 6RA

in association with

James Currey Publishers
54B Thornhill Square
Islington, London N1 1BE

Ohio University Press
Scott Quadrangle
Athens, Ohio 45701

Copyright © John Comaroff 1973, 1989 & 1990

First published 1973
First published in this edition in Britain 1990

British Library CIP Data
Plaatje, Sol T (Solomon Tshekisho), 1876-1932
Mafeking diary
1. South Africa. Politics. Plaatje, Sol T
(Solomon Tshekisho), 1876-1932
I. Title
968.04'092'4

ISBN 0-85255-068-5 (Cloth)
ISBN 0-85255-064-2 (Paper)

Library of Congress Cataloging-in-Publication Data
Plaatje, Sol. T. (Solomon Tshekisho), 1876-1932.
[Boer War diary of Sol T. Plaatje]
Mafeking diary / Sol T. Plaatje: edited by John Comaroff, with Brian Willan and
Andrew Reed.
p. cm.
Previously published as: The Boer War Diary of Sol T. Plaatje. 1973.
Includes bibliographical references.
ISBN 0-8214-0944-1 (Ohio University Press). – ISBN 0-8214-0945-X (Ohio
University Press: pbk.)
1. Mafeking (South Africa) – History – Siege, 1899-1900. 2. South African War,
1899-1902 – Personal narratives. 3. Plaatje, Solomon Tshekisho – Diaries. 4. Blacks –
South Africa – Diaries. 5. Journalists – South Africa – Diaries. I. Comaroff, John
L.,1945-. II. Willan, Brian. III. Reed, Andrew. IV. Title.
DT934.M2P4 1990
968.04'8 – dc20
89-22784 CIP
Set in 10/12pt Linotron Palatino by Goodfellow & Egan Ltd, Cambridge
Printed and bound by Villiers Publications, London N6

Contents

List of illustrations

Acknowledgements
The editors and publishers are grateful to the Mafeking Museum
for permission to reproduce photos 4, 5, 6, 7, 9, 10, 11 and 12, and
to the University of the Witwatersrand (Molema/Plaatje Papers)
for photos 2 and 8. Photo 3 is taken from H. Wilson, *With the Flag
to Pretoria* (London, 1902).

Map of Mafeking during the siege

Sunday 29th -- Divine Services. ~~there was~~
~~none.~~ No thunder. ~~Irksome~~ terror;
And I have therefore got ample opportunity to sit
down and think before I jot down anything about
my experience of the past week. I have discovered
nearly everything about war and find that
Artillery in war is of no use. The Boers seem
to have started hostilities the whole of their
reliance leaning on the strength and number
of their cannon and they are no surely
discovering their mistake. I do not think
that they will have more pluck to do anything better than what they did on Thursday
and we can therefore expect that they will either
go away or settle round us until the troops
arrive. To give a short account of what I
found war to be I can say.
No music is so thrilling and as immensely
captivating as to listen to the firing of the
guns on your own side. It is like enjoying supernatural melodies in a paradise to hear one or two shots fired off the
armoured train but no words can suitably
depict the fascination of the music produced by the action of a Maxim, which
to Boer ears, I am sure, is an exasperating
artillery that not only disturbs the ear
but also disorganises the free circulation of
the listener's blood. At the native city
of Kanya they have been entertain-
(I learn from one just arrived) with the
melodious tones of big guns, sounding a
'Grand Air' of war, like a gentle subterra-
instrument, some 30 fathoms beneath their feet and not as
                                                    remote

The first entry of Plaatje's diary, Sunday 29th October 1899.

Portrait of Plaatje (sitting, centre) and friends, probably taken shortly after the siege. Ebie Schiemann, mentioned in the diary, is seated, left.

Boer artillerymen preparing to fire their 94-pound Creusot siege-gun ('Big Ben', or 'Au Sanna' as Plaatje called it). Plaatje made a point of counting the number of shells it fired into Mafeking each day.

War correspondents in front of their dugout during the siege. Left to right: J. E. Neilly (Pall Mall Gazette, Vere Stent (Reuters), Major F. D. Baillie (Morning Post, J. Angus Hamilton (The Times and Black and White).

Barolong chiefs and headmen. Sitting, left to right: Silas Molema, Wessels Montshioa, Lekoko Montshioa. The figure standing at the extreme right is probably Mathakgong, described by Plaatje as 'one of the unsung heroes of the siege'.

The Court of Summary Jurisdiction in session during the siege. Charles Bell and Lord Edward Cecil are sitting at the desk, Plaatje, acting as interpreter, is standing alongside them. 'Myself in knickerbockers and without a jacket,' Plaatje wrote on one such occasion, 'looked more like a member of the football team or a village cyclist than a court interpreter.'

The Boer fort at Game Tree, the object of a disastrous attack by Mafeking's defenders on 26 December, 1899, which resulted in over 50 British casualties. 'Never was such a wilful suicide committed by a community in our condition,' Plaatje wrote.

Portrait of Plaatje with friends, probably taken shortly after the siege. Plaatje is standing, centre, with Isaiah Bud-M'belle, his brother-in-law, to his left.

Siege administrators, sitting, left to right: Frank Whiteley, Mayor of Mafeking; Charles Bell, magistrate and civil commissioner; Captain Greener, chief paymaster. Plaatje is standing behind, between Bell and Greener.

THE MAFEKING MAIL
SPECIAL SIEGE SLIP.

ISSUED DAILY, SHELLS PERMITTING.   TERMS :   ONE SHILLING PER WEEK, PAYABLE IN ADVANCE.

No. 72   Friday, February 16th. 1900.   127th Day of Siege

The Mafeking Mail.

FRIDAY, 16TH FEBRUARY, 1900.

OUR BEEF PROVIDERS.

The appearance of some under-cut, juicy and succulent, on certain breakfast tables made us curious in this time of Siege as to its origin. We learned it was "Native beef," and the following account, which we prefer to give in its own picturesque language, is interesting in connection with the subject of our meat supply :—

"Mathakgong, the leader of " the expedition of 10th, whose loot was captured by the enemy a fortnight ago, said he would not have a quiet night until that fiasco had been blotted out; so on Friday he took four men with him to go and make another trial. Yesterday he and his companions were coming in with what appeared to be a span (12 head) of oxen they had captured close to Batho-Batho's, near Maritzani, at 5 p.m. They brought them down safely until they reached the Magogo Valley, where the Boers fired at them. The Boers first of all fired from their right and before they had time to reply another volley came from their left. They replied calmly, but one went to the right (where the heaviest fire was) and one to the left. The Boers soon shut up but not until they had wounded two oxen. One fell amongst the Boers and one just outside our advance trench, and 10 came in safely.

"Night before last (Saturday) 12 armed Barolongs left our advance trench, South of the Stadt, to go and annoy the Boers. They crossed their lines without being observed and were only fired at on their return. As soon as they returned the fire the Boers ran back to their trench and were silent for the night."

These people attacked the homestead of a Native farmer at Maritzani and exchanged shots, but the farmer made a vigorous defence and they retired.

WHERE'S GREITJE ?

When the Boers were seen fiddling around the big gun on Wednesday and a letter under the cover of a white flag was sent in to keep us from firing while they rigged a derrick over " Greitje" preparatory to removal, some of the more hopeful took it as a sign that the damned old blunderbuss was wanted at Pretoria and that her unpleasant belch would no more twang its woeful discord on the harpstrings of our nerves. Alas, how disappointed must these optimists have been when the following afternoon the old scarifying sound was heard coming from about four miles due West instead of East, showing us that the openings to our dug-outs were all the wrong side about. However, we may comfort ourselves with the reflection that as we have borne bombarding for eighteen weeks there is no reason to funk anything these curs can do now. They have tried all the mean tricks their low cunning is capable of inventing, and now, we are nearing the end, whether they take their guns to the East or West, can make no difference to us nor to the punishment they are soon sure to receive.

The Secretary to the Sports and Prizes Funds desires to acknowledge receipt of Ten Pounds Four Shillings, being proceeds from the Concert of Sunday afternoon last.

Mafeking Garrison.

GENERAL ORDERS

By Colonel R. S. S. Baden-Powell, Commanding Frontier Force.

MAFEKING, 16TH FEBRUARY, 1900.

Court of Summary Jurisdiction.—The Court of Summary Jurisdiction will meet on Saturday, the 17th February, at the Court House, at 10-15 a.m., for the examination of such prisoners as may be brought before it. President; Lieut.-Col. O. B. Vyvyan. Member: Major F. W. Panzera.

Officer Attached.—Major Baillie, Reserve of Officers, is attached for duty (without pay) to the B.S.A. Police from the 12th instant inclusive.

Assessment Committee.—The Assessment Committee will meet on Sunday, the 18th instant, at Dixon's Hotel at 10 a.m. Owners attending at the above place and hour will be informed about what time the Committee will arrive at their respective houses.

By order,
E. H. CECIL, Major,
Chief Staff Officer.

AUCTION SALE.

THE undersigned, duly instructed by Mrs. GIRDWOOD, will sell by Public Auction on

SUNDAY NEXT,
At 9-30 a.m.

1 Pony, 1 Gent.'s Saddle & Bridle, 1 Lady's Saddle and Bridle, 1 Cape Cart, 1 Set Double Cart Harness, 2 Shot Guns, 250 Shot Cartridges, 1 Gent.'s Bicycle, 1 Carpenter's Bench and quantity of Tools, a quantity of good second-hand Gent.'s Clothing, etc.

Also 1 Black Pony (Stallion)

in the Estate of the late Corpl. Armstrong, B.S.A.P.

ALDRED & ROSS,

Government Auctioneers and Sworn Appraisers.

Don't forget the time :
9-30 A.M.

NOTICE.

A.S.C. BUTCHERY & BAKERY.

THE following hours will hold good for issue or purchase of Bread and Meat :—

5-30 a.m.	9 a.m.
6-30 p.m.	8 p.m.

No one will be served outside these hours.

Bills for Bread and Meat.—Persons purchasing privately will be required to pay cash down. There is not sufficient Staff to justify running accounts being opened.

C. M. RYAN, Capt.,
D.A.A.G.B.

Mafeking, 16th Feb., 1900.

With the sanction of the Col. Commanding

CYCLE SPORTS

(*Postponed on account of the condition of the Ground*,) will be held at the

RECREATION GROUND,

— ON —

Sunday, February 18th,

Commencing at 3-30 p.m.

Lady Sarah Wilson has kindly consented to distribute the prizes, which comprise :

Watches ; a Clock ; a most handsome hand-painted " Watteau " Fan ; Silver Glove Buttoner; Candlestick Mirror ; Silver mounted Pipes ; Amber Cigarette Holders ; Cigarette Cases, &c.

Referee : H. H. Major Goold-Adams.
Judges : Major Godley ; Capt. Cowan. Inspector Marsh.
Handicappers : Lieut.-Colonel Walford ; Inspector Browne.
Starter : C. G. H. Bell, Esq., C.C. & R.M.
Clerk of Course) To be appointed on
Lap Scorer) the Ground.

The Totalisator

Will be upon the Grounds.

Under charge of Sergt. Major Merry.

PROGRAMME :

	Start
1. One Mile Siege Championship	3-40
2. Team Race of One Mile ...	4-0
Four members of : The Prot. Regiment, the B.S.A. Police, the Cape Police, the Bechuanaland Rifles, and the Town Guard.	
3. Half Mile Bicycle Race in Fancy Costume.	4-20
One Prize for Winner, and one prize for best Fancy Dress.	
4. Half Mile Ladies Race ...	4-40
5. Three Lap Race ...	5-0
Walk a lap. Run a lap. Ride a lap.	
6. One Mile Bicycle Handicap	5-30
POST ENTRIES.	

Bicycles will be provided for those who have not their own. Lots being drawn for them.

The distribution of Prizes will take place directly after the last race.

By the kind permission of Capt. Cowan the Band of the Bechuanaland Rifles will play during the intervals.

The Mafeking Mail Special Siege Slip, *16 February 1900. The leading article ('Our Beef Providers') reproduces one of Plaatje's reports to Charles Bell about the exploits of Mathakgong, a famed Barolong cattle-raider.*

Africans queueing for horsemeat soup during the latter part of the siege.

The Mafeking Town Guard assembled for prayers on the morning of Sunday, 21 January 1900, the 100th day of the siege.

Preface

Sol Plaatje's *Mafeking Diary* is a document of enduring importance and fascination. The product of a young black South African court interpreter, just turned 23 years old when he started writing it, it opens an entirely new vista on the famous Siege of Mafeking. By shedding light on the part played by the African population of the town, Plaatje explodes the myth, maintained by belligerents, and long perpetuated by both historians and the popular imagination, that this was a white man's affair. One of the great epics of British imperial history, and perhaps the best remembered episode of the Anglo–Boer war of 1899–1902, is presented from a wholly novel perspective.

At the same time, the diary provides an intriguing insight into the character of a young man who was to play a key role in South African political and literary history during the first three decades of this century. It reveals much of the perceptions and motives that shaped his own attitudes and intellectual development and, indeed, those of an early generation of African leaders who sought to build a society which did not determine the place of its citizens by the colour of their skin. The diary therefore illuminates the origins of a struggle which continues to this day.

When the *Mafeking Diary* was first published in 1973 (under the title *The Boer War Diary of Sol T. Plaatje*), many gaps remained in our knowledge of its author's remarkable life and career, both before and after the siege. Much more information is now available. In 1984, Brian Willan's extensively researched *Sol Plaatje: South African Nationalist, 1876–1932* was published, presenting, for the first time, a detailed biography. Against this background, the *Mafeking Diary* assumes a new meaning and significance; it is now possible to read it with a far richer understanding and appreciation.

The time seemed right, therefore, to prepare a new edition. This one differs in a number of ways from the original. Firstly, where mistakes were found in the rendering of Plaatje's text itself, they have been put right. In no such instance did these corrections amount to more than a single word, name or title, but in a number of cases they did necessitate the amendment or insertion of a note. In addition, some inconsistencies in spelling, punctuation and capitalisation have been ironed out, the guiding principle throughout being to provide a text that was as accessible and readable as possible whilst at the same time remaining faithful to the spirit and intent of the original.

Secondly, some of the annotations have been amplified and many others added in the light of the new research and bio-graphical information now available. In particular, the knowledge we now have on Plaatje's life in Kimberley before he moved to Mafeking in 1898 has clarified many allusions and references to personalities he knew from this time. More generally, it has enabled us to understand far better the social and intellectual context in which Plaatje developed his character – so evident in the diary itself – in the four years before he came to Mafeking: the sense of humour, the underlying political and religious beliefs and values had all been crucially shaped during these formative years.

Thirdly, a number of substantive changes have been made to the editorial contributions. Thus the Epilogue has been expanded to include new detail on Plaatje's experiences in the immediate aftermath of the siege, while the Prologue has been modified in order to clarify the salience of events prior to it. To the Introduction has been appended more biographical material on Plaatje's youth; from it, on the other hand, has been excised a commentary, now largely redundant, upon the significance of the diary to historians, linguists and anthropologists. Finally, we have com-piled an index, which was not included in the original edition, and have included a number of new photographs.

I retain little of the original Preface, save to recount once more how the diary first came to light. The document, it should immediately be said, was discovered more by accident than by design: those among whom Plaatje lived during the siege appear to have been unaware of its existence, and I certainly heard no mention of it in any other quarter. In 1969, while conducting anthropological fieldwork in the Mafeking district, I let it be known that I should like to see any old letters or papers that families might have accumulated over the generations. Despite the absence of mass media to publicize this appeal, the news spread rapidly, and soon many items of diverse content and condition found their way to me. One particular young friend,

Victor Molema, heard of my search quite by chance; ironically, I had overlooked to ask him. Unsolicited, he proffered a tatty leather scrapbook and explained that it had once belonged to his grandfather.

As it turned out, Victor Molema was a direct descendant of the founder of Mafeking and a grandson of Sol Plaatje. Long after the South African War, Plaatje's daughter, Violet, married Morara Molema, a member of the Tshidi nobility and a son of the man with whom the diarist had lived during the siege. Before his death in 1932, Plaatje, by then an established political and literary figure, had given the Victorian scrapbook to Violet, apparently with little explanation of its content. It seems he had left Mafeking and its memories far behind.

Many years later, Violet Molema passed the scrapbook on to her son. Since last being used it had lain unopened under a pile of decaying books and other timeworn relics. It was only when he heard that documents were being sought that Victor, unaware of its contents but with a dim recollection of its source, brought it out from its ignominious resting place.

The scrapbook itself contained little of obvious interest. Occasional pages revealed scrawled notes on a variety of personal matters. But there seemed not to be much else – at least not until, holding it vertically, I tapped the edge of the book against a table to remove some of the fine dust that permeated it. As I did so, probably more vigorously than I ought to have, some sheets of foolscap slid from under the back cover of the scrapbook. Over the decades, the weight that lay on top of it had moulded it into a protective sheath for the folio on which the diary was written. Unprotected, it is unlikely to have survived in an environment in which rodents and abrasive grit destroy all but the most carefully concealed documents. The leaves on which the entries were written showed evidence of once having been bound as a note-book: remnants of blue cloth still adhered to them. The paper was brittle and yellowed with age, but the script – including, astonishingly, the passages in pencil – was almost entirely legible.

This edition has been prepared with the assistance of two colleagues, Brian Willan and Andrew Reed. Their research has yielded an enormous amount of additional information about Plaatje's life, his writings and his deeds; indeed, it is this information that has made possible a more accurate and fully documented edition of the book. Two other individuals, Mr Morara Molema and Mrs Maud Zibi, both of them interviewed by Andrew Reed, clarified many previously obscure or mis-understood references to events and personalities. It is sad they did not live to see the publication of this new edition of the diary of a man they both knew well.

John L. Comaroff, Chicago, 1989

Introduction

One fine morning I became aware of a very smart, sprucely dressed young native standing to attention before me.
'Well?' said I.
'I hear you need a secretary-typist, sir,' he answered.
'Well, so I do. Is your master one?'
'I haven't a master,' said Plaatje, with a faint smile, 'but I write shorthand and can use the typewriter.' He spoke perfect English and I engaged him at a ridiculously low wage which he named himself and seemed glad enough to get . . . I recognized, in my new secretary, an extraordinarily capable assistant. To begin with, he could spell – which I can't and never could. He was quick on the machine . . . quick witted and understanding and quick to pick up and catch a new expression, ask the meaning and the derivation of it and add it to his vocabulary. As to what would now be called a liaison officer . . . he was invaluable.[1]

Thus wrote Vere Stent, the Reuters correspondent in Mafeking during the siege and later editor of the *Pretoria News*, of his first meeting with Sol Plaatje.[2] He could hardly have foreseen, in the spring of 1899, the future that lay before his new secretary or the influence this twenty-three-year-old Morolong was to have throughout black South Africa in the next thirty years; that he would become, in the words of an American publicity sheet, 'Native African Editor, Author, Missioner and Leader of his People'.

The history of Solomon Tshekisho Plaatje's ancestors contrasts sharply with the progress of his own career. His family traced its origins to Modiboa, who is believed by Barolong to have been their eighth chief. When he died his two sons, Mooki and Tsesebe, came into conflict over their claims to the chiefship. The latter succeeded, and the former, with a group of allies, hived off to form an independent splinter chiefdom. The descendents of Mooki called themselves *Barolong ba ga Modiboa* ('the Barolong of Modiboa') in order to assert their genealogical seniority. Seven generations later, after the Barolong nation had fragmented into a number of separate political communities,[3] one of the emergent chiefs endeavoured to reincorporate the secessionists by force. As a result the *ba ga Modiboa* were scattered and compelled to seek refuge within the various Barolong chiefdoms. They were never able to re-group or reassert their political identity. Plaatje's ancestors had an early foretaste of subordination; this was to follow for most of the peoples of southern Africa in the decades after contact with Europeans. But his own personal development represents a movement to a position of pre-eminence that transcended the narrow arena of local politics. If his political objectives were national, the strategic efforts he made to achieve them were at an international level.

Sol Plaatje was born on 9 October 1876, at Doornfontein, a farm in the Boshof district of the Orange Free State. His parents were adherents of the Berlin Missionary Society, and had until recently lived at its station at Bethanie, close to the town of Edenburg. Shortly after Plaatje's birth they moved to the Society's mission at Pniel, not far from the diamond fields at Kimberley, and then part of the Cape Colony. It was here that Plaatje underwent most of his formal education, attending the church school run by the Reverend Ernst Westphal, a young evangelist newly arrived from Germany; at some point he also received instruction at the Church of England mission in Beaconsfield, part of Kimberley, from the Reverend Herbert Crossthwaite.

Plaatje remained at Pniel until early in 1894. By then he was employed as a pupil-teacher at the mission, receiving further tuition outside the classroom from Ernst Westphal and his wife, Elizabeth. Although the Westphals had been seeking ways and means of enabling Plaatje to continue his education elsewhere – the school at Pniel could only take pupils up to Standard III – he applied for a post as a messenger with the Post Office in Kimberley, an institution well known for the opportunities it afforded mission-educated Africans. He was offered the job, and commenced work there on 1 March 1894, at a salary of £72 per annum. He was seventeen years old.

The four-and-a-half years spent at the diamond fields were crucial in shaping the humorous, self-confident personality, and the precocious talent, which stand out so clearly in the author's siege diary. In Kimberley Plaatje found himself part of a well-established African mission-educated community, attracted to the town because of the availability of jobs. Most members of this community were of Xhosa or Mfengu descent; they came originally from the eastern Cape, the earliest and most successful field of missionary endeavour in southern Africa, and shared a readily identifiable set of values. Generally speaking, they were committed Christians and church-goers and believed firmly in the ideals of progress, 'improvement' and individual advancement through education and hard work. Moreover, they tended to be keen supporters of the institutions of the Cape Colony, two of which were of particular importance: the non-racial Cape franchise, which gave the vote to any male citizen who possessed property worth £75 or received an income of £50 a year, and who could fill in a registration form in either English or Dutch; and a judicial system which claimed to uphold the principle of equality before the law for all citizens of the Colony, again regardless of racial or other distinctions.

Among blacks in Kimberley these principles and values fostered a fervent loyalty to the British imperial government, to which they looked for protection and assistance in preserving their rights. The very existence of such institutionalized rights encouraged a sense of optimism about the future, and a self-confident enthusiasm for exploring to the full the opportunities which Africans, individually and collectively, saw before themselves. Nobody was to exemplify these qualities and hopes better than Plaatje, who was soon participating keenly in the affairs of the community and its busy social life. One local association came to be of special significance to him: the South Africans Improvement Society, formed in Kimberley in 1895, 'firstly, to cultivate the use of the English language, which is foreign to Africans; secondly, to help each other by fair and reasonable criticism in readings, English composition, etc, etc'. The Society then met fortnightly, and Plaatje seems to have been among its most active members.

He made his debut at its second gathering, reading a chapter from *John Bull and Co*, by Max O'Rell. The presentation was not an unqualified success: 'his style of reading and pronunciation', it was reported, 'were fairly criticised'. But his contribution to another meeting a month later, when he read a paper entitled 'The History of the Bechuanas', was rather better received: 'Being a Bechuana', we are told, 'he showed great mastery over his subject'.

Plaatje was also a diligent reader in private, and developed a particular fascination for Shakespeare, whose plays he went to see performed at the Kimberley Theatre. At the same time he studied a number of languages with a view to securing a position as court interpreter. In this he seems to have been inspired by the example of his close friend Isaiah Bud-M'belle, an Mfengu, with whom he for a while shared lodgings. A clerk and translator in the Griqualand West High Court, Bud-M'belle (mentioned several times in Plaatje's diary) was himself a man of immense ability and wide-ranging talent. Plaatje himself was soon fluent in English, Dutch, Xhosa, German and Sesotho, as well as his own native tongue, Setswana. It was not long before he was contemplating a more rewarding and challenging occupation.

Before the right opportunity came along, however, Plaatje made one other important decision. In January 1898 he married Elizabeth M'belle, Isaiah's younger sister. Inter-tribal marriages such as this were the accepted thing in the cosmopolitan African community in Kimberley, but this was certainly not the case with the two families concerned, and both were initially strongly opposed to the match. Once presented with a *fait accompli*, however, they soon came to accept what was to be a very happy marriage.

Later that year Plaatje found the career opportunity he had been looking for. The post of clerk and court interpreter fell vacant in Mafeking, some 200 miles from Kimberley, and he applied. After an interview he was offered the job, accepted and commenced his duties on 14 October 1898.

* * * *

Plaatje was no stranger to Mafeking. He had visited the town on several occasions in the late 1880s and early 1890s, and his father had moved to a farm in the district several years previously. Indeed, Plaatje himself was already sufficiently well known to the *boo* Molema, one of the leading families among the Tshidi-Barolong nobility, to be able to secure from Silas Molema, its senior elder, a recommendation for his new job. Molema believed that a young man of such education and ability could be useful both to his own family and to the chiefdom as a whole. His advocacy undoubtedly helped to convince Charles Bell, the local magistrate and civil commissioner, of Plaatje's suitability for the post. The latter involved interpreting in the magistrate's court when it was in session, and acting as a clerk and translator of documents when it was not. In 'The Essential Interpreter', an essay written some years later, he makes it clear that he greatly enjoyed the work, took his duties seriously, and soon became highly proficient. Certainly Bell was pleased; in April 1899 he noted that Plaatje was 'a steady, diligent person', to be trusted in every respect, and a great improvement upon his predecessor, Andries Jan Moloke.

Plaatje himself was keen to make the most of his new opportunity. During the first half of 1899 he studied for a number of Cape Civil Service examinations, hoping thereby to qualify for promotion and an increased salary. In August, he wrote off to register for the tests in Dutch, German and Typewriting. Although he was sent the necessary registration certificates some weeks later, they never arrived: on 11 October, two days after Plaatje's twenty-third birthday, Mafeking was surrounded by Boer forces. The British imperial government and the two Boer republics were at war.

The fact that Plaatje wrote a diary during the siege was probably unknown to most of his friends. Except for a single mention in an obscure formal affadavit,[4] he seems not to have referred to it subsequently. Survivors of the siege who were familiar with the author at the turn of the century did not recall it; nor do others who came to know him later. It may not have occurred to him to keep a journal at first. But it is highly likely that he followed the example of the many people around him who started writing them as soon as the siege began: the newspaper correspondents, the army officers with whom he was in close contact and, above all, Charles Bell, whose diary Plaatje was then asked to type. In these circumstances it would have been surprising if the notion of maintaining his own had not suggested itself to him; in addition, he might well have perceived it as a convenient way of exercising the novel phrases over which he questioned Vere Stent and others so carefully. From the manner in which the journal was kept, and its obvious tone of privacy, it is clear that Plaatje had no thoughts about publishing it. Certainly he appears never to have made any effort to do so.

* * * *

Sol Plaatje's career as a public figure began in 1902 when he assumed the editorship of *Koranta ea Becoana* ('The Bechuana Gazette'), a bilingual newspaper financed by Silas Molema. Over the next decade he emerged as a leading spokesman for African opinion and, in 1912, became the first secretary of the South African Native National Congress (forerunner of the African

National Congress). In particular, he was a vocal and active participant in the struggle against the disabilities imposed upon blacks after the Union of South Africa in 1910, especially by the Natives' Land Act of 1913. This act was among the most significant in the history of South Africa. A long and complicated piece of legislation, it provided, in essence, for the creation of 'scheduled native areas' in which Africans could own land: outside these areas they were specifically barred from the future purchase or hire of land from anyone other than an African; within them Africans could not sell to non-Africans. Plaatje objected to the law on several grounds. In the first place it would leave vast numbers of black tenants on white-owned farms with a choice between eviction and servitude (which was permitted under the Act). Secondly, the 'scheduled native areas' were of grossly insufficient size; and, as they were generally held corporately by lineages, clans or chiefdoms, the notion that individuals would be able to buy land was nonsense. Indeed, the legislation, far from fostering African advancement would encourage 'tribal' consciousness and foster cleavage in an age when the black élite was encouraging the emergence of a national identity. But, most important of all, Plaatje foresaw this as a major step towards the dispossession of African rights, a triumph of repressive Afrikaner republican ideas on 'native policy' over the Cape liberal tradition. 'Awakening on Friday morning, June 20, 1913,' he wrote, 'the South African Native found himself, not actually a slave, but a pariah in the land of his birth.'[5]

Plaatje devoted his energy, time and his modest resources to the fight against the Act. Immediately after it was passed, he toured South Africa in order to investigate the effects of its implementation. In his report, first presented orally at SANNC meetings and then published in *Native Life in South Africa*, he argued that the legislation had angered and upset a considerable number of whites as well as the blacks who were more immediately and drastically affected; and it would seriously damage any hopes of mutual understanding and *rapprochement* in the future. Throughout he emphasized what he believed to be 'Dutch' inhumanity towards rural Africans, recording the plight of his people with a sense of dignity and pathos that makes the book an especially eloquent and moving polemic.

After a SANNC delegation appealed unsuccessfully against the Act in Cape Town in May 1913, Plaatje urged the leadership to send representatives to Great Britain in an effort to persuade the imperial government to support their protest. But here, too, the emissaries – this time Plaatje among them – met with stoic refusal; His Majesty's Government thought it undesirable to interfere in the internal affairs of South Africa. Reminders of African loyalty during the Anglo-Boer War, of former assurances of political protection, went unheeded. The outbreak of the First World War put an end to any hopes that the delegation might still have entertained. But Plaatje himself exploited to the utmost his period abroad: on every possible occasion he addressed public gatherings – usually under the auspices of religious organisations – in order to rally public opinion. In addition, he wrote and published *Native Life in South Africa*. Both the book and the speeches consolidated his image as the leading spokesman for his black compatriots, a reputation with which he returned home to South Africa in 1917.

In 1919 Plaatje led a second Congress delegation, and on this occasion managed to secure an interview with the Prime Minister, David Lloyd George. Lloyd George was impressed by their case, and wrote about it to General Smuts, the South African premier; but there was never any prospect that the British authorities would take direct action to remedy the grievances of the Africans. Plaatje then took his campaign to the United States, this time alone. In an attempt to interest black Americans in his cause, he addressed hundreds of meetings and left a deep impression upon the people he encountered; still, he failed to raise any money for the social and educational work to which he was now keen to devote himself, and returned home in 1923, forced to accept that there was no likelihood of outside intervention on behalf of his people.

Throughout the 1920s, earning his living as a journalist, Plaatje continued to speak out in defence of black rights; in so doing, he added his voice to many others seeking to dissuade General Hertzog, now the prime minister, from implementing his policies of segregation. Plaatje's own political influence was no longer what it had been, however. Having emerged as a national leader in the years prior to the First World War, he was never fully able to come to terms with the massive transformations brought about by rapid industrialisation in South Africa. He had always emphasised the importance of individual uplift and moral regeneration for his people, and was active in the temperance movement, but there was little he could do to influence a hostile government. The sense of optimism so strongly evident earlier on, and especially in the Mafeking diary, gave way to a grim pessimism about the future.

The last few years of Plaatje's life are best remembered for his literary endeavours. In 1930 he at last found a publisher for his English novel *Mhudi*, which had been completed ten years previously; his Tswana translation of *Comedy of Errors* was also published, and was the first African-language version of Shakespeare to appear in print. But much other work remained unpublished, and many of his manuscripts were lost. In the early 1930s he was working on, amongst other things, a Tswana–English dictionary, a compendium of Tswana praise poems and folk tales, a number of other translations of Shakespeare's plays, and a new edition of the collection of proverbs (*Sechuana Proverbs and their European Equivalents*) which he had first written in London during the war. Few South African writers possessed Plaatje's depth of vision or facility in its different languages and cultures.

Sol Plaatje died in Johannesburg on 19 June 1932, and was buried in his home town of Kimberley. The composition of the congregation at his funeral bore testimony to his career as a public figure. South Africans of all ethnic groups – family and friends, representatives of church, government and press – heard eulogies of which Plaatje, the 'eloquent advocate of Native Rights',[6] himself would have been proud. In the weeks that followed, newspapers in South Africa and the United Kingdom recalled, at great length, his many-sided achievements. For, despite the growing accusation that he had become too 'Europeanized' and hence less militant than of old, there seems to have been an awareness that his death robbed the African national movement of a respected negotiator, a powerful voice and a versatile littér-ateur. One obituary, written by a devoted friend, summarized the emotions that Plaatje seems to have evoked in his followers:

> A great, intelligent leader; a forceful public speaker, sharp-witted, quick of thought, critical; a leading Bantu writer, versatile, rich and prolific; a man who by force of character and sharpness of intellect rose to the front rank of leadership notwithstanding the fact that he never entered a secondary school. . . . Never have I found him autocratic, contumacious, or narrow of outlook. Whatever subject he touched upon . . . was treated with a brilliancy, humour, ability and finish that at once surprised and captivated, inspired and humbled me. . . .[7]

Those attuned to more dispassionate assessments of deceased statesmen might find this somewhat excessive. Yet, with hindsight, it is not difficult to understand why Plaatje inspired such admiration. This was an era during which black South Africa still believed that the future of their country could be influenced, at least to some extent, by their own constitutional actions. Energetic activists like Plaatje not only embodied the dream, but appeared as the instrument of its fulfilment.

Prologue

The story of Mafeking begins early in the nineteenth century, many years prior to the establishment of the town itself. Before the white settlers had begun to leave the coast of southern Africa and move deeper into the hinterland, a series of so-called 'tribal' wars, occasioned by the rise of Tshaka's Zulu state, had set the indigenous African populations in motion, and the chain reaction of belligerent campaigns reached into the furthest corners of the subcontinent. The Barolong chieftains, who had formed a single 'nation' (*morafe*) until c. 1780, found themselves in the midst of the resultant confusion as they were attacked by the Matebele of Mzilikazi and the Batlokwa of Mma-Nthatisi in turn. The Tshidi-Barolong, who lived then in the Molopo plain on what is now the South Africa–Botswana border, took refuge alongside the other Barolong at Thaba 'Nchu, some 250 miles south-east of their homeland.

The Tshidi spent some seven years at this refuge, remaining there until 1841. During this period, a band of Voortrekkers under Andries Hendrik Potgieter visited the stronghold and were, by all accounts, hospitably received. A few months later, after they had settled on land given them by a nearby Bataung ruler, the Voortrekkers were attacked and dispossessed of their stock by Mzilikazi's regiments. Potgieter despatched his brother to the Barolong chiefs who, on hearing of the Boer plight, sent them cattle. The alliance so established was further consolidated when the two parties combined to defeat Mzilikazi and put him to flight; or so it seemed to the chiefs, who had the firm impression that, in return for their efforts, their right to their ancestral lands would be acknowledged – despite Potgieter's grandiose claim, by right of conquest, to much of central southern Africa north of the Orange River.

Thus, when the Tshidi returned to the Molopo, in 1848, after a long series of migrations, they assumed that their territorial rights would not be questioned. But the Boer leaders had not intended this at all, and a protracted series of disputes ended the

15

alliance and mutual goodwill. When the Tshidi chief, Montshiwa, refused to acknowledge his servitude to the newly independent Boer republic of the Transvaal, he was told either to join its forces in battle against the Bakwena, another recalcitrant Tswana chiefdom, or to face the consequences. He refused and, in 1852, before the threatened 'punishment' could be fully effected by the local Boer commander, fled with most of his people to Moshaneng in Bangwaketse country. But this refuge, some sixty-five miles north-west of Mafeking, was remote and imposed limits on Montshiwa's strategic control of the Molopo region. Realizing that occupation is nine-tenths of possession, the exiled chief sent five of his brothers, each with a small following, to create a ring of settlements aimed at forestalling the westward expansion of the whites. One brother was directed to establish a village along the Molopo river. He chose a site in the centre of the claimed territory and named it the Place of Rocks, *Mafikeng*, in recognition of its predominant topographical feature. This brother, Molema, was the leader of the small Christian congregation in the chiefdom and his despatch also removed a potential internal threat to the unity of the polity. Molema and his small band reached their destination early in 1857.[1]

The sites chosen for the ring of settlements were chosen primarily for their defensibility, a wise decision as it later turned out. For however strongly Montshiwa complained of Boer encroachment on his traditional territory, the Boers were equally vociferous in claiming that the Tshidi had no right to retain this land at all. It is unnecessary to follow the three decades of acrid debate over the matter. Later, when verbal aggression led to the outbreak of hostilities, Montshiwa himself moved to Mafeking and – at the insistence of Molema – established his capital there. The little village became the centre of the Tshidi universe; and, as it did so, it assumed symbolic importance for the Boers who resented the chief and his attempts to persuade the imperial government to aid him in thwarting the expansion of the Transvaal. Thus Mafikeng represented British thorn in the side of Boer aspiration. And Montshiwa was bitterly resented for his part in this.

Matters came to a head in 1881 when a junior Barolong chiefdom, the Rapulana, who had been attacked by the Tshidi and driven off their land, recruited aid from a third Barolong grouping and a number of European freebooters and drove Montshiwa out of one of his strongholds, Dithakong. The 'peace' concluded after this incident dispossessed the chief of a considerable portion of land, some of which was given to the Europeans, who founded the Republic of Goshen. But the cessation of hostilities did not last long, and the Goshenites and Montshiwa were soon at war again. On the advice of Cecil Rhodes, then the resident of the British government in Bechuanaland, Sir Charles Warren was sent in 1885 with a force to 'restore order . . . and to defend the Native tribes who had placed themselves under British protection'.[2]

Under the name British Bechuanaland, the imperial government annexed the territory 'north of the Cape Colony, south of the Ramatlhabama spruit and Molopo river, west of the South African Republic.'[3] It was then that Sir Sidney Shippard, who was appointed Administrator, Chief Magistrate and Supreme Chief of the Natives created the settlement of Mafeking about a mile from Montshiwa's court. Thus there are two adjoining towns: Tshidi *Mafikeng*, and its later-established European counterpart, the name of which is a corruption of the original.[4] Their co-existence, and the events which led to it, explain – at least in part – why the siege occurred. It is true that, for the Boers, Mafeking was a convenient point from which to commence their offensive on the western front when the South African War broke out on 11 October 1899. Yet its ultimate strategic importance is questionable. Indeed, it has been argued that the Boers made a grave error in committing a large force to a 217-day siege which, even if successful, would have yielded a relatively modest military return; that they could have by-passed the town and deployed their troops more profitably elsewhere. But, for them as for the British and the Barolong, Mafeking represented the confluence of competing interests in South Africa at the time; its significance was more than merely logistic.

In the fourteen years since the establishment of Mafeking (as opposed to *Mafikeng*) a community of about 1 500 had developed – a neat little railway centre of diverse population. By then transferred to the Cape Colony,[5] the town had been built around a spacious market-square with the municipal offices in the middle. The new Victoria Hospital and convent constituted its northernmost buildings. Apart from railway installations, Mafeking could already boast many communal facilities: a race-course and a recreation ground, a courthouse and gaol, schools, churches, a masonic hall, hotels, a bank, a library and several shops.

In anticipation of the war, Colonel R. S. S. Baden-Powell had

arrived in southern Africa in July 1899. His orders were to raise
two battalions and train them, and to take charge of the Rhodesian
and Bechuanaland Police. Moreover, he was warned to be discreet
about his activities for fear of antagonizing not only the enemy,
but also those allies who were afraid that any military preparation
might be construed as an act of aggression. Most of the training
took place at Ramatlhabama, across the Bechuanaland Protectorate
border. Here, too, Baden-Powell, as officer commanding the
North-Western Forces, decided to split his strength and to despatch
a regiment (under Colonel Plumer) to Tuli on the Limpopo river;
the defence of Rhodesia was also his responsibility. Until Sep-
tember permission for the newly-trained corps to move into
Mafeking was withheld; but eventually the Cape authorities
relented and allowed an armed force to be placed in town to
guard the stores that had arrived by rail. Baden-Powell promptly
transferred the entire garrison, for the order had not specified
any particular number of men. Even in Mafeking their activities
were kept secret from the townspeople, though the Mayor, Resident Commissioner and Resident Magistrate were drawn into
the covert preparations. Above all, they feared the presence of
Boer spies in the town, for the population included several
families of Dutch descent.

By the time that the siege was laid, the populace of Mafeking
had been divided into several contingents. The Mayor, Mr F.
Whiteley, officially called for men to join a Town Guard, and
about 300 enrolled. A group of so-called coloureds made up a
sixty-strong corps of 'Cape Boys', while the Black Watch was
composed of recruits who, being non-Barolong, lived in the
'strangers' location' outside the town. One hundred railway
employees organized themselves into the 'Railway Volunteers'.
The Tshidi, while not forming a separate contingent, provided a
number of volunteers who were variously deployed during the
siege. These civilians manned the inner defences of the town,
and served as a labour force.

The militia itself consisted of four detachments: the Protectorate
Regiment (21 officers and 448 men), the Bechuanaland Rifles
(5 officers and 77 men), the British South African Police (10 officers
and 81 men) and the Cape Police (4 officers and 99 men). This
garrison of 745 soldiers was mounted and armed with Lee-Metford
rifles and, when they ran short, obsolete Martini-Henrys. Artillery
support was bound to be scanty: apart from four outdated seven-
pounders (all muzzle-loading) the total armoury comprised a

one-pounder Hotchkiss, a three-quarter-pounder Nordenfeld, seven Maxim .303 machine-guns and two small quick-firers.

The defence installations were no less crude. Although small forts were being built and linked to Baden-Powell's headquarters at Dixon's Hotel by field telephone, it was a long time before an effective network of barricades and protective structures established Mafeking as a tightly knit stronghold.

The bleak situation at the start of the siege was ameliorated by the arrival of an armoured train, a highly mobile and effective weapon. Hastily garnered stores of dynamite, although limited, were also to be a significant factor in the defence. Still, none of this did much to offset the reported Boer strength. While it is difficult to ascertain the exact size of the besieging force – which, in any case, fluctuated over time – there appear to have been periods when the British were outnumbered by eleven to one. Organized into 'commandos' which were recruited by district, the Boers were mounted, carried Mauser rifles, and were well supplied with ammunition. Their artillery included at least ten modern pieces of various sizes, apart from a ninety-four pounder that reached Mafeking towards the end of October.

Baden-Powell, after reviewing the situation, became convinced that it was advisable to include the Tshidi-Barolong *stadt* in the invested area if the Boers besieged the town. The morality of this decision has been questioned, but from a purely military point of view it was undoubtedly a wise one. According to Plaatje,[6] the Tshidi were themselves quite explicit about the desire to participate in the defence:

> The Barolong and other native tribes near Mafeking were keenly interested in the negotiations that preceded the Boer War. The chiefs continually received information regarding the mobilization of the Boer forces across the border. This was conveyed to the Magistrate of Mafeking with requests for arms for the purpose of defence. The Magistrate replied each time with confident assurance that the Boers would never cross the boundary into British territory. The Transvaal territory is only ten or twelve miles from the magistracy. The assurances of the Magistrate made the Natives rather restive; the result was that a deputation of Barolong chiefs had a drar·atic interview with the Magistrate, at which the writer acted as interpreter. The chiefs told the Magistrate that they feared he knew very little about war if he thought that belligerents would respect one another's boundaries. He replied in true South African style, that it was a white man's war, and that if the enemy came, His Majesty's white troops would do all the fighting and protect the

territories of the chiefs. We remember how chief Montshiwa and his councillor Joshua Molema went round the Magistrate's chair and crouching behind him said: 'Let us say, for the sake of argument, that your assurances are genuine, and that when trouble begins we hide behind your back like this, and, rifle in hand, you do all the fighting because you are white; let us say, further, that some Dutchmen appear on the scene and they outnumber and shoot you: what would be our course of action then? Are we to run home, put on skirts and hoist the white flag?'

Chief Motshegare pulled off his coat, undid his shirt front and baring his shoulder and showing an old bullet scar, received in the Boer–Barolong war prior to the British occupation of Bechuanaland, he said: 'Until you can satisfy me that His Majesty's white troops are impervious to bullets, I am going to defend my own wife and children. I have got my rifle at home and all I want is ammunition.'

Baden-Powell, like the magistrate, stressed that this was to be a white man's war.[7] He asked for Tshidi co-operation in so far as their village would be included within the lines of the invested town, but claimed not to be keen that they take up arms. The inclusion of the *stadt* did mean, of course, that a larger population had to be fed. But the commanding officer must have known that the Tshidi were widely reputed for their cattle-raiding ability, a useful skill in the anticipated circumstances. When, later, the war of attrition took its toll, the fact that local blacks were rationed more severely than the townspeople, and that death by starvation was rife among them, did not affect his determination to hold out; nor did it alter his view that the Tshidi would have been worse off in Boer hands. Both Baden-Powell's critics and his supporters seem to agree that he expected, desired and sought to provoke a siege. And both have based their assessments of his subsequent behaviour on this presumption.

Thus the irrevocable decision to include the *stadt* was taken, and it certainly affected the nature of the siege. Oral tradition among the Tshidi has it that, although most were in favour of supporting the former allies of Montshiwa, they were far from convinced of the military strength of the garrison. Apart from all else, they remembered the British defeat of 1881 at the hands of the Boers. But, as the diary indicates, they turned out to be faithful allies.

This, then, was the scene in Mafeking at the outbreak of the war. Almost immediately after the commencement of hostilities, Baden-Powell declared the suspension of civil law in favour of a martial régime and despatched Colonel Hore and his Protectorate Regiment to a position on the eastern heights to await the Boers. Twenty-four hours were to elapse, however, before the first shots were to be fired – by the armoured train at a party of horsemen.

During the first week one serious battle was joined. For the most part, fighting was restricted to sniping and artillery bombardment. During this early period the terms of confrontation were tacitly laid down by Colonel Baden-Powell and General Cronje, the two commanding officers.

One cardinal rule was obeyed by both sides for most of the 217-day siege: there was to be no firing or any form of belligerent activity on Sundays. However bitter the battles of the week had been, the Holy Day was to be observed. Furthermore, there was to be no firing on the Red Cross flag flown atop the mule-drawn ambulances that entered the scene of the battle once the soldiers had withdrawn. In addition, Baden-Powell requested Cronje not to direct fire at either the convent, occupied by the Irish Sisters of Mercy, or the Victoria Hospital. Later, when a camp was set aside outside the town (but within the lines of investment) to accommodate women and children in a spot safe from the shelling, immunity was sought for this as well. From time to time the agreement broke down, and such incidents were invariably followed by lengthy correspondence.

During these first days the attention of the garrison and the citizenry was devoted to improving the defences within the six-mile perimeter of the besieged area. For example, a minefield, which was three-quarters dummy and one-quarter dynamite, was laid to reduce as far as possible the number of front-line troops required. Similarly, the British South African Police (BSAP) camp across the railway line from town and to the north of the *stadt*, was more strongly fortified. It is clear that the limitation of hostilities to relatively mild shelling facilitated the effort to prepare Mafeking for its coming trials. But the situation changed radically on 24 October, when the ninety-four pound Creusot siege-gun began shelling from the Boer *laager* at Jackal Tree. The next day the garrison had to repel an attack from the south-west, for the enemy believed that its artillery bombardment had significantly weakened the defence. Another threatened onslaught expected on the twenty-sixth never materialized; and on the following night Baden-Powell ordered a counter-attack on a strong fortification to the east of the town. In so doing he assumed some initiative in a not unduly optimistic situation. That the Boers planned another offensive was taken for granted. It was simply a matter of guessing the time and the place. This is the point at which Plaatje begins his entries.

CHAPTER 1

October–November 1899

Sunday, 29th

Divine Services. No thunder. Haikonna[1] terror; and I have therefore got ample opportunity to sit down and think before I jot down anything about my experiences of the past week. I have discovered nearly everything about war and find that artillery in war is of no use. The Boers seem to have started hostilities, the whole of their reliance leaning on the strength and number of their cannons – and they are now surely discovering their mistake. I do not think that they will have more pluck to do anything better than what they did on Wednesday[2] and we can therefore expect that they will either go away or settle round us until the troops arrive.[3]

To give a short account of what I found war to be, I can say: no music is as thrilling and as immensely captivating as to listen to the firing of the guns on your own side. It is like enjoying supernatural melodies in a paradise to hear one or two shots fired off the armoured train; but no words can suitably depict the fascination of the music produced by the action of a Maxim, which to Boer ears, I am sure, is an exasperation which not only disturbs the ear but also disorganizes the free circulation of the listener's blood. At the city of Kanya[4] they have been entertained (I learn from one just arrived) with the melodious tones of big guns, sounding the 'Grand Jeu' of war,[5] like a gentle subterranean instrument, some thirty fathoms beneath their feet and not as remote as Mafeking; they have listened to it, I am told, with cheerful hearts, for they just mistook it for what it is not. Undoubtedly the enrapturing charm of this delectable music will give place to a most irritating discord when they have discovered that, so far from it being the action of the modern Britisher's workmanship going for the Dutch, it is the 'boom' of the state artillerist[6] giving us thunder and lightning with his guns.

I was roaming along the river[7] at 12 o'clock with David[8] yesterday when we were disgusted by the incessant sounds and clappering of Mausers to the north of the town: and all of a

sudden four or five 'booms' from the armoured train quenched
their metal. It was like a member of the Payne family[9] silencing a
boisterous crowd with the prelude of a selection she is going to
give on the violin. When their beastly fire 'shut up' the Maxim
began to play: it was like listening to the Kimberley R.C. choir
with their organ, rendering one of their mellifluous carols on
Christmas Eve; and its charm could justly be compared with that
of the Jubilee Singers[10] performing one of their many quaint and
classical oratories. But like everything desirable it ceased almost
immediately. The Maxim is everybody's favourite here. Whenever there is an almost sickening rattle of Mausers you can hear
them enquiring amongst themselves when 'makasono' is going
to 'kgalema'.[11] Boers are fond of shooting. They do not wait until
they see anything but let go at the rate of 100 rounds per minute
at the least provocation. I am afraid if they could somehow or
other lay their hands on a Maxim they would simply shake it
until there is not a single round left to mourn the loss of the
others. One can almost fancy that prior to their leaving the State[12]
their weapons were imprecated by empyrean authority – and the
following are my reasons for believing that the State ammunition
has been cursed: when I passed the gaol yesterday afternoon
Phil[13] told me that while some prisoners were working in front of
the gaol one of them was hit by a Mauser bullet (from the Boer
lines) on the ribs. They expected the man to drop down dead,
but the bullet dropped down (dead) instead. Immediately after,
another hit a European's thigh. It penetrated the clothes but
failed to pierce his skin; and just as if to verify this statement,
another came round and struck the shoulder of a white man, who
was shocked but stood as firm as though nothing had happened,
when the bullet dropped down in front of him.

I have already mentioned that on Wednesday (the day of the
all-round attack) I was surprised to find that on getting to town
not one person was killed – while the Dutch ambulances were
busy all the afternoon.

On Friday morning Teacher Samson[14] and 15 others crept
along the river until they were very close to a party of Boers, who
were busy sniping the location[15] from an ambush. They killed
eight of them and wounded several; they were all going to return
without a hitch – but they advanced to disarm the dead men, and
Samson received a slight wound on the shoulder.

Yesterday 22 Fingoes[16] went out to the brickfields,[17] which
may be said to be exactly on 'disputed territory': they took

shelter among the bricks and killed several of them, which vexed the latter to such an extent that they fetched one of their 7-pounders and cocked it right into the kilns. Our men lay flat against the bricks, 7-pounder shells crashing amongst them with the liberty of the elements. They went for the bricks, knocked spots out of the ground they lay on, and shattered the woodworks of their rifles between and alongside them; in fact they wrecked everything except the flesh of human beings. It affused several of its mortal discharges over them and when convinced that every one of them was dead, cleared away leaving the 22 men quite sound, but so badly armed that if the Boers had the courage to come near they would have led them away by the hands. The gunsmith is very busy mending their rifles, two of which are quite irreparable, and the men are having holidays in consequence.

Our ears cannot stand anything like the bang of a door: the rat-tat of some stones nearby shakes one inwardly. All of these things have assumed the attitude of death-dealing instruments and they almost invariably resemble Mausers or Dutch cannons. We often hear the alarm and run outside to find nothing wrong; and such alarm was often the motion of the pillow if one was lying down. David was yesterday grumbling: 'Oh, what a restless life; if I knew that things were going to turn out this way I would never have left Aliwal North.'

After I left Mr Mahlelebe yesterday I came through the gaol yard onto the Railway Reserve's fence. Mauser bullets were just like hail on the main road to our village. I had just left the fence when one flew close to my cap with a 'ping' – giving me such a fright as caused me to sit down on the footpath. Someone behind me exclaimed that I was nearly killed and I looked round to see who my sympathizer was. When I did so another screeched through his legs with a 'whiz-z-z-z' and dropped between the two of us. I continued my journey in company with this man, during which I heard a screech and a tap behind my ear: it was a Mauser bullet and as there can be no question about a fellow's death when it enters his brain through the lobe, I knew at the moment that I had been transmitted from this temporary life on to eternity. I imagined I held a nickel bullet in my heart. That was merely the faculty of the soul recognizing (in ordinary post-mortal dream) who occasioned its departure – for I was dead! Dead, to rise no more. A few seconds elapsed after which I found myself scanning the bullet between my finger and thumb, to realise that it was but a horsefly.

It is very difficult to remember the days of the week in times of war. When I returned from the river[18] early this morning I found David still in bed, and he asked me if there is any sign of their advance. He was dumbfounded when I said that they were not likely to advance as today was Sunday. What, Sunday? He thought it was Thursday (Ha! Ha!).

Monday, 30th

During this day we received another ultimatum[19] that if we did not surrender we would be bombarded early next day. We knew that the big gun had been with us for more than a week, and as she failed to shake us in eight days I am afraid that the Boers are merely fooling themselves to imagine that we entertain any fear in being bombarded – for so far from being alarmed, we are getting used to it. I look back to reflect on the slight damage caused by these shells, nearly 200 of which have already been wasted on the town. Considering the expense of one of them (opinion on this point differs, some saying £35 and some £47), she[20] is really not worth the fuss. Meanwhile the position of the big commando at Lothlakane[21] is being moved down the river to a spot about three miles west of here, and one from the eastern to another spot three miles to the north.[22] We are anxiously waiting to see what tomorrow's day will bring forth.

Tuesday, 31st

Long before 5 o'clock we were aroused by reports of Ben[23] going as rapidly as she did last week. She was accompanied by the enemy's 7-pounder and all other pounders. We woke, dressed in a hurry, and went to the rocks to find things really very serious at Makane.[24] They were shelling Makane and the dust was simply like a cloud around our little fort. The Boers were advancing towards the koppie like a swarm of voetgangers:[25] they came creeping under cover of their shells, which were flying over their heads and preceding them like a lot of lifeless but terrific vanguards, until they opened fire with their muskets at long range. Their fire was very heavy, for the whole of the Dutch army had come from all round Mafeking and turned their attention towards our little fort at Makane. They have evidently discovered that to capture the whole place at once was a hopeless task and they had therefore decided on capturing one by one of our forts until they have nipped every one of them in the bud.

As there was no chance of any bullets coming round my way

I had a fair chance of admiring the whole of the proceedings. The stadt had such an advantage over the situation that it was quite impregnable amongst the trees in the Molopo – while the surroundings are a wide, wide plain which one can examine from the rocks without being observed. That is one reason why Montsioa held out against the Boers for so many years.[26] He had only been defeated once, and that was when the tribe had their headquarters at Sehuba[27] before Mafeking was the capital.

To return to the subject. I think I have already stated that the Boers attributed their failure to the fact that we never leave our trenches to give them a chance of tackling us in the open. This morning they must have thought that they would easily compel us to do so by weakening Makane and naturally getting us to run to her assistance, thereby affording them an opportunity of going for us in the plain between this and there. If this was their expectation they were sorely disappointed, for nobody cared.[28] They went for the little fort from east, south and west with muskets and artillery, the former being volleys from about 800 hands. But nobody in town, or anywhere else, troubled his soul about it. The volunteers round the place, seeing that all of the guns were turned towards Makane, stood up and admired the operation as though it was a performance on a theatre stage. It must have given them a headache to find such a multitude of them advancing towards a fort occupied by 70 officers and men of the B.S.A. Police[29] – and nobody caring to go to their assistance. But this was not all: the enemy came quite close and still not a shot came from within the mysterious little fort. I believe the Boers (who always let off a number of rounds unnecessarily) must have thought that everyone was dead, for nearly 20 tons of bombs had already been plugged into the fort. The fortifications looked quite old and ragged in consequence. All of a sudden there came volley after volley from the dumb fort and we could see them fall when the Maxim began to play; some dead, some wounded and some presumably to wait until dark.[30] Their officers, who were mounted behind them and urging them on, were – with one exception – the first to run and at 9 o'clock they hoisted the Red Cross. Their ambulances and Natives were busy 'tutaing'[31] till about midday. Our losses were two officers and five men killed, and six wounded.[32]

This engagement was very unfortunate to me as it deprived me of one of my dearest friends in the place, in the person of the Hon. Captain Marsham. These experienced soldiers never care

how fast bullets may whizz about them: they stroll about in a
heavy volley far more recklessly than we walk through a shower
of rain, and that is how he wrecked a career that was going to
give him a name almost too heavy for his youth.[33]

The enemy having had the reverse of this morning's attack, we
had a very quiet day.[34]

Wednesday, 1st

Nothing happened during the day but in the evening my dear
friend Mr E. G. Parslow was murdered by Lieut. Murchison –
mentioned in the official publication yesterday.[35] This murder[36]
has not only deprived me of a good friend but it has wrecked me
financially. He paid for my little assistance[37] so liberally that I
never felt the prices of foodstuffs that [have] reigned here since
the commencement of the siege. The cause of the murder is
incomprehensible; but then reasons are hardly tangible.

Thursday, 2nd

Nice and pleasant rains.[38]

Friday, 3rd

We have on this day received more shells than on any other
occasion since the 25th ultimo. But we are gradually getting used
to them and it is getting more like a holiday than a siege.

Saturday, 4th

A shell burst near the church this morning and a fragment hit a
Kgalagali's[39] arm, which was amputated – poor fellow. A Mauser
bullet hit one Mrs Graham at the women's laager.[40] She was
taken to the hospital where she is doing well.

Sunday, 5th

Guy Fawkes' day. The usual prayers and thanksgivings. Late
last evening about 1 000 Boers were seen crossing from the
southern laars[41] over to the north of the town, but as it soon
became dark we lost sight of them. Just about the time 'Au
Sanna' always fires her 'bad-night'[42] shot we heard the report
coming from the north instead of the south; we, however, thought
little of it as it might have been that our ears were mistaken. This
morning, however, it was discovered that it was a dynamite
explosion that went off.

The railway line being on a gradient a few miles north of the town, the Boers filled the trolley with dynamite, tied a fuse to it, lighted the fuse, and pushed it down the reclining line into town. Their intention was apparently to wait until the dynamite exploded somewhere about the railway station and killed everybody, when they would walk in and then publish to the civilized world that they had taken Mafeking at the barrel of the Mauser. But God forbade it and their determinations had been frustrated. The dynamite exploded a half-mile beyond the graveyard, smashed the trolley that carried it, tore up the line and blew up the ground.[43] While some of us were paying homage to the All-Father in places of worship, some were busy arranging the line to prevent a re-occurrence. A very fine day. Soft and pleasant rains till eve.

Monday, 6th

'Au Sanna' gave us beans in the early morning and at about 8 o'clock she was moved from her old post to about two-and-a-half miles south-east of the town. They must have got a scent about the arrival of the troops and are temporarily stationing her there, preparatory to her departure – if it is not for the purpose of getting a better command of the town. She gave her début at her new quarters at 3.30 in much the same humour and vigour as near Jackal Tree.[44]

Twenty Barolongs[45] under Paul[46] went to accompany 80 whites, who went to annoy the burghers of the laar down the river. More than 80 volunteered to go but on learning that they were not going to fetch the Dutch cannon which causes a great deal of annoyance from the west, all but the twenty got disgusted and declined to proceed on an errand with such a trifling design.

I find it easy to count Sanna's shots every day and will put every day's numbers in brackets after the date.

Tuesday, 7th (15)

Early this morning we were woken by the rattling of muskets and artillery to the west, and specially pleasing was the 'bub-bub-bub-bub-bub' of the Maxim in accompaniment – and the whole affair bounced along and echoed away among the ridges in the distance in splendid harmony. The whole of the procedure was so entertaining that I felt I will not have cause to regret it when our men come back.

Meanwhile we could see them heliographing half-way between the two laagers and we know they were calling for reinforcements.

Shortly after, a force of about 600 mounted Boers could be seen circulating around our range and making for the scene of operations. Our men got there in the dark and waited until they could see the tents very clearly, when they started peppering volley after volley in the middle of the camp, which was soon enveloped in a thick cloud of dust – and some Boers [were seen] running away half-dressed. They continued to fire while they retreated slowly and the twenty of our people who accompanied the party said that everything was executed in grand style. They only regretted when they saw the Boers running away and leaving their big gun about 100 yards this side of the camp. They thought if there were enough of them they could have made straight for the gun and captured it, despite any European orders to the contrary. For it was only when the Boers saw that they were being reinforced that they came back to return the fire. All this caused the loss of eight of our horses shot, one volunteer severely and three slightly wounded. Master Bell's[47] horse was among the killed. It was shot whilst he held it by the bridle. Later on we saw two ambulances busy. We spent a quiet day afterwards.

(Except that a shell burst in the hospital and considerably excited the patients. A letter was sent to Cronje,[48] remonstrating and telling him that.)[49]

Wednesday, 8th (10)
Thursday, 9th (10)
An occasional 'boom' from a piece of the state artillery kept us in memory that we are beleagured. Otherwise all week pleasant rains the order of the day.[50]

Friday, 10th (8)
A Dutchman finished his term of imprisonment today. He was taken from gaol direct to Weil's store,[51] where he saw, no doubt, that there was plenty of food in Mafeking. He was provided with his own choice in tinned food, biscuits and etc. – just as many as he could carry. He was blindfolded and sent across the line.

Saturday, 11th
Today we had a shell at 6 a.m. and another at 10.30 and 'Au Sanna' never moved since. Oh, how we wished that she should be silent for good. We were only molested by the thinner artillery during the day, but those are not of much account.

Sunday, 12th

We have a black Sherlock Holmes in the person of Manomphe's son, Freddy. He arrived from Kanya with some despatches this morning in company with Malno's brother-in-law: the latter was on horseback, which is very risky to cross the enemy lines with.[52] On Friday the horseman remained behind and Freddy came across a party of 60 Boers at Tlapeng.[53] He hid the letters and went straight up to them. They searched him for letters, and on finding nothing on his person, they became very friendly – more so when one of the party recognized him as an old good servant of his. They gave him a quantity of mutton which he roasted on the spot and had a fine repast at the same time as his Dutch friends. They left the place at 5 p.m. giving him an opportunity of fetching his letters. He reached his home (Ga-molimola)[54] in the evening and hid his letters in an ant-heap close by. Our friend the horseman, who met no Boers, arrived the same evening. Freddy advised him to return to the bush and hide his horse all day next day (yesterday) until dark, when they would plan the best way of getting into town. Freddy became doubtful of the man's aptitude and requested him to hand over his letters to him for safekeeping, which he did.

In the morning a party of 40 Boers rode past Modimola and asked Freddy where the cattle were. Subsequently another party (of 90 this time) also came past. After leaving Freddy's place, this last party observed the spoor of a horse. They traced it to a small village a little beyond. (Instead of going to where Freddy showed him, our foolish friend went to this village.) When the inhabitants perceived the party approaching along the horse's spoor, they decided to give them to understand that it belonged to the owner of the village,[55] and that his son had been riding it looking for stray goats. There was an interpreter of some sort who promptly advanced to meet the ephemeral conquerors of Mafeking and related to them the history of the horse. The head of the village – the old fool – overheard this, and blurted out that he was lying. This infuriated the Boers, who sentenced the interpreter to receive 55 cuts with a stirrup leather for his lies, and made a prisoner of our foolish friend while the interpreter was undergoing the sentence. When Malno's brother-in-law got arrested he whined and begged the Boers not to take him alone as he was not the only offender: there was another man, ahead with the Magistrate's letters, and they came from Kanya together.

The Boers returned to Freddy, who lied so classically, and with such thoroughness and serenity, that they disbelieved their prisoner's statement. They searched his person, his house, nay everything, but failed to find them; and Freddy walked calmly in here with both despatches this morning. From Freddy's information, the reason why we are having such quiet days is because the Boers have gone in different parties to loot our stock. We hope that by the beginning of next year they will be purging them back to us in much the same manner as they did 14 years ago.[56]

We spent this day in church. The pulpit was occupied by Mr Lefenya,[57] who warned his hearers to be very careful in their prayers, and remember that their God was the enemy's God; we, however, have the scale in our favour as we have never raised our little finger in molestation of the Transvaal Government, or committed an act that could justify their looting our cattle and shooting our children in the manner they are doing. The weather was fair and as shelling and Mausering were conspicuous with their silence, we wished that Sundays would come a little more often.

Monday, 13th (2)

The enemy having gone to Kgoro, Phitshane etc.[58] to steal our cattle, we had a very quiet day. Only two shells came in from 'Sanna' and Mausers not quite a thousand.
(Shelling slow and Mausering mild.)[59]

Tuesday, 14th (2)

Not a single shot during the forenoon. Lovely showers set in in the evening. And altogether one fairly concludes that life is really worth living, even during a siege.

Wednesday, 15th (3)

Pleasant soft rains all day today. Some fighting in town without any results on our side. The cause of the abrupt decrease of our daily supply of 'Sanna' shells may be that they are running short of ammunition or that last Friday's Dutchman told them that the thing is doing us no damage meriting the expense and fuss they have in firing it. I have never had a shell burst near me, but this afternoon while I was at the residency[60] one of them exploded somewhere to the east. A fragment came along, found its way through the roof, across the ceiling, hit the opposite wall and dropped on the floor. This was in one of the rooms, but I thought that the whole house was coming down on me and I could already picture to myself a number of volunteers picking up fragments of my body and piecing them together preparatory to them being laid in the grave. This, however, did not come to pass, for then I would not have been able to write any notes on the occurrence.

Thursday, 16th

Heavy rains fell during the night, and they continued somewhat pleasantly all day today. This will soon [mean] a great improvement to the stock in the place as they are not permitted to go more than a mile for food. Besides, there are so many of them that the ground in the neighbourhood of the camp was quite naked. Bechuanaland grass, after a rain like this, takes a very short time to grow and by this day next week we will have the country as green as a garden. This, and the undoubted nearing arrival of the troops, will render Rantho'akgale's[61] dream of starving us out an impossibility. A 7-pound shell from the east burst near the railway bridge: a piece of it came all the way from there and struck the pate of a piccaninny[62] in the stadt. He bled very much but is expected to get through.

Friday, 17th (17)

What a lovely morning after yesterday's rains. It is really evil to disturb a beautiful morning like this with the rattling of Mausers and whizzes and explosions of shells. 'Au Sanna' appears to have been sharpened up, for her fire was very vigorous and quick since 3 o'clock. Mausers were also very brisk today. Goodness knows what these Boers are shooting: they kill on average only one goat, sheep or fowl after spending 5 000 rounds of Mauser ammunition – but very rarely a man. Thick clouds came up during the afternoon and by sunset we had very heavy rains. One of 'Sanna's' shells entered the sitting room at Riesle's new Mafeking Hotel and played havoc with the furniture. Mrs Graham, who was shot at the women's laager on Saturday the 4th, was in the hospital and progressing favourably: a fragment of a shell that burst near the recreation ground entered the hospital and frightened her so much that she broke one of her blood vessels and died in consequence. She was a young widow and leaves three little chickens to fight life's battle without parents. 'Sanna' was very sharp today, firing every three minutes instead of eight as heretofore. She has either got fresh ammunition or a fresh gunner.

Saturday, 18th (4)

What a pleasant morning. One often wishes that it could be mutually agreed that both sides should lay aside their guns and go out picnicking, and not resume operations until Monday morning, January 1st, when the troops will be in the country for certain. When I reached the rocks, I found the people arguing over the meaning of the unusual movements of the people in the laager down at Koi-koi.[63] My field-glasses discovered that it was the enemy trekking, from one neighbourhood towards Lothlakane. Oh, how we wish them God-speed and a safe departure across the border. Everybody is so pleased at the laager dispersing that very little attention is paid to Big Ben's outbursts. I went out for a ride for the first time since the siege; enjoyed it so much that the sun set whilst I was still on horseback.

We have just got definite information that the troops landed at Cape Town on the 4th instant and that they are given six days rest prior to proceeding north. There is a general dismay in fool's paradise where their movements were not being studied before telegraphic communications were cut between this and the civilized world. Bets were freely entered that they would be here on the 30th *ultimo*, then the Sunday after, etc., etc.; and bets are still pending that they will be here day after tomorrow. I have the honour of not sharing this dismay for, having expected them to reach here on the 20th, I prolonged my period to the middle of December, when October went past and we had heard nothing of their whereabouts.

The prices of foodstuffs ran up to a very high degree: meat from 10d to 2/0d per pound, bread from 1½d to 6d a loaf, and groceries and other necessaries in similar proportions. The office closed the stores on 12th *ultimo* and did not even open to pay us at the end of the last month: the probabilities are that we will receive October's pay together with November's and December's at the end of the year, as relief appears to be as far as ever. The forage also rose from 4d to 1/6d per bundle but I was lucky enough to get free Government rations from the military authorities for our pony, who now feeds on Scotch hay and oats – and he is as fat as a slaughter-pig. He has, since the siege, been working only with his teeth and I think it is his wish that Mafeking should be besieged a little more often: this, and the fact that I keep pace with the hard times by means of earnings from newspaper war correspondents[64] who (though not quite like my late lamented friend)[65] are fairly liberal, are good reasons why I should sing the twenty-third psalm.

Sunday, 19th

I have forgotten to mention that some time ago the church bells, which were heretofore used for no other purpose than to remind the public that it was time to worship their creator, have been turned to some other service; they ring in case of an alarm.[66]

The church bells, which have always been a comfort to Christians, are now a nuisance as they signify the advance of the enemy. During the first week of hostilities the alarm was sounded by a bugler, galloping from one end of the camp, blowing the bugle with all his force, while others echoed the strain to all corners of the camp. Since the arrival of this big thing[67] galloping is an impossibility and the church bells are substituted. One has to depend on this timepiece for Divine Service, which we very seldom attend as we do the whole week's work today. But in spite of all that the humiliation, prayers and thanksgiving offered to the All-Father are of such far greater sincerity and deliberation than on an ordinary occasion.

It sounds much like a sabbath morning when after six days of terror and shuddering (as though one had no right to live in this world) one has the liberty of breathing freely and enjoying the calm atmosphere, which gives the Sunday a more different and blessed aspect than the other days of the week. Saints and sinners alike thank God for the leisure and wish that there were three Sundays in every week.

David trampled the back of a big snake with his booted foot last night. When the brute made for his leg he picked up a stick and killed it.

The Government have started a cheaper grain store for the benefit of the poor in the stadt.

Monday, 20th

Wireless telegraphs brought news that Cronje with his 3 000 men had been recalled, by orders from Pretoria, to reinforce the south.[68] He left the Marico burghers under Malan and Botha to look after us. The big gun was broken, and another arrived on Friday from Pretoria, to relieve the broken one.[69] It is the intention

of the remaining Boers to continue shelling until the inhabitants
are reduced to eating horses (sick vanity), which they are sure to
do as the Boers are able to stay around for a year or two. An
American[70] who carried Reuter's despatches from here on Saturday last slipped safely through the Boer lines.

'Au Sanna' was very brisk this morning, hardly giving us any
time to dress and wash our faces.

Mrs Mahlelebe carried her 'drag' with great pleasure during
these trying times and was yesterday delivered of a son – much
to our relief. We can now commend both mother and son to the
care of the All-Father with the hope that the heavy and menacing
experiences of the past four weeks will not affect the life of the
little one.

We are continually being cheered by news from the Natal
border. This is so interesting that we always forget our strain in
congratulation of our forces there. How we would cheer if we
heard similar reports from Kimberley. Altogether more shots
were fired than on any day since the 25th *ultimo*. 43 all told; this
from the big gun only.

Tuesday, 21st (6)

About 50 shots from the thinner artillery and 30 or 40 times
that number of Mauser rounds in what we call a quiet day.[71]

Wednesday, 22nd (8 × 2)

All of the smaller artillery, except one 7-pounder, appeared
to have left us and it is therefore easy to mention the total
number of shots that visited us each day. The number 8 × 2
at the beginning of the first paragraph in each day's notes
represents the number of shots fired by Sanna and the 7-pounder
respectively.[72]

Thursday, 23rd (10)

St. Leger's[73] birthday. The weather fair and cloudy but occasional
dust just prevents one from calling it a lovely morning.

Mr Molema[74] and I did our best to find a fattish sheep to
slaughter in honour of the occasion but like everything in a siege
we were only able to find one after a hot day's search.

The day was the hottest since the spring but soft rains refreshed
us in the afternoon. We wished him joy and hoped that his next
birthday would find him between both his mother and father
and not in a similar state to this, when the distance and the

enemy between (and with broken means of communication) completely debar one from sending him and his mother a congratulatory wire.

I was interpreting for the Officers' Board for the second time last night. I will be at it again this morning at 9.00 and tonight at 7.00.

One is always wondering whether or not a shell from 'Au Sanna' will not smash up the roof and crush our brains.

Such courts, however, transact a lot of business in a very short time as evidence is taken by a shorthand writer, which causes one to extremely enjoy interpreting, as you have to fire away without stoppages.

The authorities have since the siege been in the habit of 'gaoling' everyone (principally Dutchmen) suspected as a spy or of treasonable conduct. While there were a good many of them they planned the best scheme of how they could lock up the gaol guards, murder the balance, and clear out; like all lawless schemes this reached the ears of the authorities and they were promptly brought to book. A gaol guard named Walker brought trouble upon himself by being associated with this party. The order says: William Walker, describing himself as a Scotchman, but preferring to express himself in Dutch, was charged with treason, but in the absence of an efficient and qualified Dutch interpreter, was remanded.[75] I have since joined the Court of Summary Jurisdiction.[76]

Friday, 24th[77]

Hardly anything worth mentioning beyond the usual rattling of Mausers and boom of cannons.

Saturday, 25th

The summary jurisdiction courts are not as particular as our divisional courts about punctuality. Night before last I was warned to be at the office at 7 p.m. I misunderstood the warning and went to the courthouse until they sent for me half-an-hour later. Last night I was told to be at the office at 6.15. I misunderstood the time this time and turned up at 7.00. I thought that these warriors would pistol me as this was my second offence but they viewed the matter with total unconcernedness. This morning I turned up ten minutes late. The shorthand writer was also 15 minutes late. The officers, finding me an irresolute, unreliable wobbler, engaged the services of a white man as the witnesses

and prisoners were principally Boers – but the fellow being an
amateur interpreter was completely flabbergasted when it came
to cross-examinations, and I took his place to immense advantage.
This lateness appears to be a disease with which I am infected
and I will see it does not occur again as I feel very uncomfortable
in consequence.

This evening they gave me an opportunity of realizing what it
is to wait for others. We all turned up at 6.15 sharp but the
presiding officer failed to put in an appearance. At 7.20 he was
sent for and his excuse was that he had forgotten all about it. My
patience was so exhausted that I would have knocked him down
if I had the means. I was very restless in court, for 'Sanna's' 'bad-
night' shot always comes between 8.00 and 9.00 p.m. The court
was over at 8.55 p.m. When I left it flashed through my brain that
'Sanna's' close-up[78] is always directed towards the town. I, however, had my doubts and wondered if this evening they may not
prefer to knock spots out of the B.S.A. camp. Then the whole
plain I was to traverse would just lie in the course of the shell. I
ran in order to cut quickly across this risky ground. I had no
sooner reached the outskirts of the stadt when a big red flame
was visible to the east – and imagine my joy of the forethought,
for around came the usual row, then the loud hum which turned
to the side of the town and went to knock bits of brick out of the
B.S.A. buildings. Thank God I ran and it didn't fly over my head.
(7 × 2)

Sunday, 26th

A lovely morning, no thunder; only prayers and thanksgivings.
I sneaked the following from the Civil Commissioner's diary
today:

> Boers come out of their trenches and sit in long rows on the
> embankment and gaze upon Mafeking with covetous eyes and they
> no doubt marvel at our holding out so long, after five weeks of
> continuous shelling. They cannot understand what has become of
> us as they never see anyone: and the rat-tat of the Maxim and
> pop of the Lee-Metford are the only sounds emanating from this
> mysterious town.[79]

Distant howls in the Dutch Reformed church told that they
held service there for the first time today. About 40 people went
to the English church: when there was much danger only four
people went and now that there is practically no danger, 40 go.

Surely the people of Mafeking are merely eye-servants of the Lord.[80]

Malno left today for Kimberley. Gave him messages to Pniel and Kimberley.

Monday, 27th
Nothing worth mentioning. (13 × 11)

Tuesday, 28th
Last night a party of Barolongs were working at the town defence works. 'Sanna's' 'bad-night' came round at 9 p.m. and burst just near them. Killed one, seriously wounded two and a fourth was but slightly wounded. If every one of these shots were to bag as much as this one there would surely not be a single fellow alive as the number spent on Mafeking is now between three and four hundred.

Wednesday, 29th
A fine morning. The hot summer sun in the east, with dark moving clouds in the west, indicates rain. It is quite easy to walk in town today. The Dutch snipers being conspicuous with their silence, one walks with the privileged liberty of a fellow in Jones Street, Kimberley. Instead of the usual blood-stirring clapper of Mausers we are having that music so delightful to the ear when our guns are firing.

Captain FitzClarence was this day determined to give the Boers 'no show'. He went out to a little fort that has just been made beyond the location, which places the big gun fairly within musket range. At first he would allow them to load – then fire a volley at them. They (the Boer gunners) dispersed each time the gun was loaded and about to discharge a shot. He afterwards disallowed them even to come near her at all, firing at them every time they approached; practically making it bitter for them to approach their own gun. These things are not very beneficial to us as it is very hard to kill any of them. Still they are good as they show the Boers that they are not going to have things all their own way and this accounts for the nominal figure which represents our supply of today.

We had heavy rains since 6 p.m. It is still raining and is likely to continue all night and probably all day tomorrow.

Yesterday there came news for the *Mafeking Mail* that the Boers crossed the Orange River bridge, Norvalspont, on the 4th instant, and occupied Colesberg; that others crossed the Bethulie bridge and destroyed the lines across the Orange. This is the line for Burghersdorp where my little family is and I can now simply commend them to the care of the All-Father; as Bud and the Judge President are most likely cut down below,[81] they will decidedly be in his care. All this is very puzzling. We had heard up to the end of October that Burghersdorp in particular was quite safe – but this was very embarrassing. This morning there came a despatch (official) and threw a different complexion on the situation entirely: that the Boers attempted to cross the Orange River and found it impassable. One could almost fancy that yesterday's news was from across the border for it not only cast gloom on our side but also added that the troops, who have done such splendid service a little while ago on the Natal side of the Transvaal border, are now falling back to Estcourt and that the Colenso camp is smashed up in consequence (bad news). The whole of the country between the border and the Tugela is proclaimed Free State territory. It now remains for us to judge whether we have to believe the *Mafeking Mail's* service, or the official despatch, as the difference between the two is so great. I would, however, prefer to believe the official service were it not accompanied by the following blood-stirring execrable lie: 'The big gun at Mafeking, weighing ten tons, cannot be worked on account of heavy recoil.' Fancy sending trash to people who are under constant thunder from the gun that cannot be worked. The truthful – or truthlessness – of both puts us exactly between the devil and the deep blue sea, if it does not remove relief as remote as ever.

Thursday, 30th

Early this morning Captain FitzClarence was at it again and declined to give the Boers opportunity of coming near their own gun. This must have enraged them very much as they tried to approach in large numbers and knock the cheek out of our few naughty snipers. They were quickly silenced and we enjoyed that sweet and enchanting music from our musketeers. It gave us an entertainment of the sweetest music imaginable when slow volley after volley was directed at the angry Boers: now and then a 7-pounder would harmonize the proceedings with an occasional 'boom' in sweet bombardment, and the whole of the proceedings is as safe as an altar.

EDITORIAL NOTE

The diary entries composing this chapter coincide with a distinctive period in the progress of the siege itself. Under General Cronje the Boer forces made a number of direct attacks on the town. The intention of the Boer commander was to bring about the defeat of Mafeking as quickly and as completely as possible. The advantage held by the Republican forces both in manpower and in arms made this a realistic possibility. The beleaguered garrison was quite aware of this, and Baden-Powell prepared his strategy accordingly. His comparatively small fighting-force could not afford defeat in the field, being hard put to man the perimeter of the besieged area. At the same time the Commanding Officer knew that to allow his enemy complete initiative would have been disastrous both for reasons of morale and of logistics. Thus he planned quick thrusts at the Boer lines on the basis that, whatever happened, his forces should always have a line of retreat. It was a policy of harassment without involvement. That this succeeded is proved by the fact that morale in the town was high as sortie after sortie forced the Boers to retrench.

In the meantime defences in the town were being improved. A ring of forts (in telephone contact with Baden-Powell's headquarters at Dixon's Hotel) provided a constant watch on the perimeter, while trenches and redoubts sheltered the townspeople from the dangers of heavy shelling. Careful assessment of the food situation had proved encouraging, for nobody at this stage expected the siege to last 217 days. If it were possible to question the besieged citizenry about their hardships they would probably have suggested that – other than the sorrows contingent upon the deaths of close friends – lack of news and feelings of isolation were perhaps the most irritating of all.

A crucial event in the history of the siege was the departure of Cronje. With his replacement by Snyman the entire picture altered. Until the 18th the much respected General had caused the defenders many a headache, for he planned to vanquish Mafeking through direct attack. Snyman, on the other hand, adopted a far more passive – and pessimistic – approach. He relied on artillery bombardment – and time. Under him the Boer forces began the long wait; starvation appears to have been the fate which Snyman planned for his enemy. The wisdom of this approach seems questionable on purely strategic grounds – for this type of investment required a large number of men that might well have been deployed elsewhere; in a war on a territory as large as South Africa's mobility was crucial. Many have suggested that in adopting this position, Snyman did precisely what Baden-Powell had hoped for. This argument implies that the British military authorities wanted the siege to continue – at least until reinforcements arrived from England. For this would solve their problem of deployment in the face of a larger force, at least temporarily. Such extrapolations are easy to make in retrospect; they concern the broader issue of the allocation of forces across the country. The relevance for the people of Mafeking was more fundamental: it meant that, although they had to tolerate shelling, they could worry more about the problem of succour and somewhat less about the prospect of military defeat. True, it was necessary to be on constant guard; but the relative lull following Snyman's arrival allowed an opportunity for the organization of the community, both civilian and military.

CHAPTER 2

December 1899

Friday, 1st

A very lovely morning after the last two days' rain. I have lately said that all of the small artillery appears to have left us, but I see that in this I was grossly mistaken as the one-pounder Maxim is sounding out there and there are two other 7-pounders besides the one that had always been there. We had trying entertainment from the whole lot, but they are not of much account.

Saturday, 2nd

We received a lot of news today – by people from across the border and also from a despatch-rider. The latter is Freddy No. 2. He is a member of the Lefenya family and was out to Kuruman.[1] On his arrival there he found the Cape Police in the Seoding camp, beleaguered. The missionary (Reverend J. T. Brown), who had the 'Vierkleur'[2] waving over his dwelling-house, would not even look at him, but drove him away directly he learned that the man was from Mafeking and absolutely declined to tell him which was the safer way into the Boer-surrounded camp. He, however, delivered his despatches and on his way back called at Ganyesa,[3] where he was caught and searched by the Boers, who on finding these letters on him took him to Vryburg. They reached there in the night and he escaped under cover of the dark while they were busy reading his despatches. He returned to Ganyesa that very same night and on the following day interpreted for his pursuers in an interview with Chief Lethlogile.[4] The Chief, on being asked with which side his sympathies were, said he sympathizes with no one and was quite neutral from the fight but he was only going to side with the winning side at the end of the trouble – clever fellow.

The smaller artillery round us have just arrived. I wonder whether the Boers still imagine we are afraid of the 7-pounder, for the lot of them put together are not half, nay, even quarter, of 'Au Sanna'.[5] Therefore after six weeks under 94-pound shells it is folly to think any number of 5- and 7-pounders would knock anything out of us.

From across the border we learn that it is quite true that we silenced two of the enemy's guns on the 23rd[6] and that the following is the result of the season's fixtures between Baden-Powell's 400[7] and Cronje's 10 times that number:

Baden Powell   287   What a licking!
Cronje   19

Mind you, this does not include the fight on October 14th and the bayoneting on October 21st. Those games were against the Snyman and Botha teams called the Marico commando – exclusive of Cronje who only fought on the occasion of the all-round attack of October 25th, the attack on Makane on October 31st and the morning of Tuesday 7th *ultimo*.

P.S. I have allowed Cronje too much: he did not score 19. 7 were scored by the Marico laager, 7 by Cronje at the Makane game – 31st October – and the big gun is responsible for the balance.

Sunday, 3rd

This is the Lord's day. All deadly instruments have been laid aside and we are now thinking of the goodness of the All-Father and his immeasurable wisdom in preserving for himself the seventh day that all men should worship. I wonder how we should be if that was not the case. When the week rolls past and we find ourselves alive on Friday morning we congratulate ourselves as we will only have two days more before the blessed sabbath, on which we will get rid of the horrible thunder for a day. There is only one thing we are particular about and that is not to stray too far from within the 'lappie-grond'[8] forming the perimeter of Mafeking between us and the enemy's lines, as this is disputed territory. It is really touching to see ladies and children from the women's laager (where Mr F. Whiteley, the Mayor,[9] had been their Good Shepherd for all the week) meet their brothers, husbands, fathers, etc. from the trenches. From Monday to Saturday our beleaguered home has the appearance of Judgement Days, while today it looks like a gay Christmas. There were all kinds of sports today; gymkhana, turf, band and concerts.

Monday, 4th

When I reached town this morning I found that despatches had arrived. They bring news of Kimberley having been successfully relieved[10] on the 23rd *ultimo*, by a force of 3 000 troops and that Lord Methuen was coming up with ten thousand more men.

Kimberley, which we thought had been relieved about a month ago, had only just been relieved on St. Leger's birthday. He was surely going to have a grand birthday if he happened to be there.

We had only three shots from 'Sanna' in the forenoon and none in the afternoon. While still jotting down these notes I looked at my timepiece to find that it was 9.33: 'Sanna's' 'bad-night' always came between 8.00 and 9.00 so I was saying to David that the old dame is not going to 'lumelisa'[11] today.

I had hardly finished when 'bang' went a terrible report, a sharp loud hum, and then a blood-stirring explosion and other reports when the deadly fragments proceeded to complete their various missions. This is an abominable life.

There is an item about Linchwe[12] having surprised a lot of Boers, captured cattle, horses, wagons, Mausers and a lot of women. The latter were returned to their sweethearts as surely as aught else was detained. Women are not of any value in war. Only Boers view the subject differently. Kgakgamaco[13] and Senobe[14] were coming from Modimola the other day and were fired on by Boers. Only the previous week some women were coming in from the same place. They carried bundles on their heads and the Boers shot a bundle off one head. The stubbornness of Barolonghazi[15] is extraordinary. They stopped, picked up the bundle and calmly loaded it again. 'Baka ba bolaea fela.'[16]

An officer of the Protectorate Regiment sent his wife to Mosita for safety. She afterwards went to Setlagoli as Boers were visiting Mosita almost daily. She subsequently found Setlagoli intolerable and decided to go up to the Boers and ask them for a permit to come in to Mafeking. The Boers detained her at the laager and sent word to Baden-Powell that they could only release Her Ladyship provided one Petrus Viljoen (a prisoner undergoing nine months' hard labour for theft) is allowed to go to the laager. I wonder what will be the end of the correspondence.[17]

Tuesday, 5th

I had a busy time today. A white man was charged with committing rape on a Native girl. The police rescued her off him and made a prisoner of him. I interpreted in this case and just when the evidence was about to reach the filthiest, superior authorities (military) demanded my services and I departed only to return towards the conclusion when the interpreting in it had become quite ceremonious. The military court cares nought for any such cases: I believe we will keep the evidence until the roads are open and commit him for trial before the judge next quarter.

I did not return to town this afternoon, the heaviest rain of the season having graced us with a visit. Surely if things go on at this rate the few, with whose ploughing the effects of this war did not interfere, will have too much grain for house consumption. The shower was heavy but quiet – so quiet that I fell asleep and only woke at 4.10 p.m. to find the village in flood. As I happened to be away in dreamland, and do not know what took place, I will leave the *Mafeking Mail* to describe the affair:

Dead puppies, stinking sprats, all drenched in mud, drowned cats and turnip tops came tumbling down the flood' is what Dean Swift said in his description of a city shower. We suppose from his mentioning dead puppies and drowned cats that he meant it was raining 'cats and dogs'. We don't know the origin of the 'cats and dogs' shower but, if its root is 'kata doros' as some learned writer suggested or 'contrary to experience' we think it rained 'cats and dogs' yesterday. A sprinkle of over eight inches in about one hour is decidedly contrary to experience. Fortunately we are so positioned that there is ample natural drainage to take away even the enormous quantity of water which fell yesterday, but the trenches were soon filled and from them the water could not run. More damage to property was done by the storm than the Boers could ever accomplish in their 'storming'. Rations were destroyed, kits washed away, and in one case a man was nearly drowned, or smothered in the mud. He slipped in, fortunately feet downwards, and had not two of his companions been near him and promptly 'hauled him back again' he would have been done for. At the hospital redan[18] the underground kitchen was flooded with six feet of water, the dinner beef spoiled and various little 'extras' the men had subscribed to buy, were lost. The women's laager trench was an underground canal. The sisters[19] were washed out from their 'bomb-proof' and the Cape Police had an hour's diving in the seven feet deep coffee coloured pool for Maxim ammunition; while everyone had an experience of wetness and discomfort, which it is to be hoped will remain unique, but which was borne by the whole garrison in the same cheery manner which has been shown during all the time of the siege. We hope our friend the enemy enjoyed himself, and to help cheer him up we should like to tell him that through his lack of nous and pluck he missed a chance yesterday to annoy us, which is never likely to present itself again.[20]

Some people had been over to the Boer lines to 'thiba'[21] cattle. They managed to get four – abnormally fat elephants. They gave one to the chief, slaughtered two, ate part of the meat, and retailed the balance. I did not avail myself of the opportunity of finding out what loot tastes like as Meko had slaughtered a fat hammel and the hard ox is not very desirable when palatable mutton is knocking about.

Wednesday, 6th

Went to town for a while in the morning then visited the Meko's,[22] whose children are very ill. At 3 p.m. I went to see Vere Stent[23] on business. He left the hole and we settled for a chat in the open air when we were unsettled by a loud bang just at old Gerrans' blacksmith shop exactly opposite where we were. We looked and saw things mighty gloomy in the blacksmith shop: grown-up folks screaming in the dark smoke like piccaninnies after 'kgoathaing',[24] while old Gerrans could be seen walking about in front of the shop, his face as black as that of a corner man in McAdoo's Vaudevilles.[25] It turned out to be an explosion of an originally unexploded shell, which had been picked up and sold to someone and the purchaser, like all others, took it to poor Mr Gerrans to empty the fuse and the powder. Mr Gerrans had been doing many of them and as there are exceptions in all cases, this particular one stood no molestation but burst with the vigour of a shell direct from 'Sanna', knocked poor Mr Gerrans' left-hand fingertips off, blackened his face with powder, tore his trousers and vests to pieces besides 'other wrongs and injuries'. As for Mr Green his assistant, it went for his leg (its favourite part) so severely that it had to be amputated; but an unfortunate person, a refugee from Johannesburg named Smith, happened to be passing in front of the scene of this outburst just at the time of the explosion and had both his legs so fearfully battered that he was only able to scream at the start. When I reached there he lay quite quiet and the poor fellow died shortly after.

One shell hit Mr Weil's store yesterday. The store was full of customers and shop employees. It entered through the roof, travelled between the roof and the ceiling, shattering the beams until it destroyed the ceiling and exited through the wholesale door. Fragments made a race for the railway station. During that race a Burghersdorp chap – a refugee from Johannesburg – came in contact with one and was killed. The crowd in the shop escaped without injury. Another shell came round in the afternoon. It entered the private house of our young Town Clerk, pierced the outer wall and went on to a room in which the Town Clerk was. It destroyed the room and wrecked everything inside except the Town Clerk – a marvellous escape: one fragment went to the kitchen, where the cook, a very stout bastard[26] lady, was and shook her so vehemently that she nearly had the perfect circulation of her blood disorganized.

Thursday, 7th

A lovely morning. After I got up I rode in the direction of Meko's to enquire where last night's shot fell, as it burst in the stadt. I found that it had fallen on the ground near a wagon wheel to which a cow was tied, whence the broken shell made for the cow, despatched it to eternity, splintered the strong wagon and severely wounded a chappie that was playing on the other side of it. Bits of the cow's meat were scattered in every direction. When I was there, shelling proceeded very briskly from 'Sanna' and the smaller artillery which are of minor importance. Only 'Sanna' is our 'ingwe'.[27] I went up to town and just after I crossed the railway line, the alarm bells chimed. The pony knows them already and he became infuriated and bucked like a dam cow while I tried to make him stand on the lee of Whiteley, Walker & Co's store. He was still bucking when a shell flew overhead with a sharp loud hum and burst in the direction of the railway. Things were too serious to permit of a fellow hanging about the streets of Mafeking and I turned round the stadt way as fast as his legs could carry me. The next shell burst just as I reached the outskirts of the village.

During my short stay in town I learned that the first shell of this morning burst near one of the railway cottages and killed a young fellow by blowing off his belly and pitching his intestines onto the opposite roof.

The man Phil-june[28] has been allowed to go so Lady Sarah Wilson reached here this morning. She says the Boers at the laager say that their forces are slaying thousands of the English everywhere – at least so they are told – but they are puzzled as to how Lord Methuen managed to reach Kimberley if that was the case.

I wonder why the Boers are so 'kwaai'[29] today. During the last few days we seldom had a 'Sanna' shell during the forenoon, and then a day's complement was only between two and four, but this morning we had seven between 7.00 a.m. and 8.00 a.m. from

'Sanna' only, besides a heavy thunder from the smaller artillery and a shower of Mausers which played the accompaniment. The middle of the day was somewhat quiet but operations were resumed at 3.30 p.m. with great vigour. I was obliged to stop going to town this afternoon despite urgent private affairs. The afternoon fire lasted till sunset but 'Sanna', just to show that she is older and mightier than the lot, kept up her part as long as the moon was shining – till 8.30 p.m. It will be a serious business if the Boers are going to give us no more sleep while the moon is shining. We always had only one shell – the 'bad-night' shot – fired into us between 8.00 and 9.00 p.m.

This single one we find very inconvenient as it makes everyone imagine, at sunset, that he is either going to have his legs shattered or a few nambulatory[30] escapes – if he is not annihilated to death; but if we are going to have them as regularly as we had them this day we might as well expect to be throwing up the sponge soon. Our patience is altogether exhausted. When the trouble commenced no one dreamt that we would still be beleaguered at the end of November: others gave the troops only up to 30th October to arrive here; I, however, gave them up to 30th October to reach Kimberley and to arrive here on 20th November, which was the most liberal of the lot. But here we are today, December 7th, losing people daily and not even able to tell where the troops are. Surely if everybody knew that this was going to be the case we would never have had the forebearance to start it. The result of yesterday afternoon's 'Sanna' outrage was two whites and a Native killed, and two whites wounded. If we are going to die at this rate I am sure there will only be wounded people hopping about single-armed and with amputated legs to tell the history of the siege.

One of the killed was in Mr Riesle's bar (Mafeking Hotel). They are dead against our poor ex-Mayor. When they shelled us with 12- and 7-pounders, on the 16th October, Mr Riesle was the only person who got his windows smashed; I have already described how they went for his sitting-room and wrecked the piano and goods therein being, but have not mentioned that when 'Sanna' (before she was christened) gave her début in Mafeking on October 23rd Mr Riesle was the first victim. It went for him in a quaint manner; some flames had to be put out, which has never been the case with any other explosion up till this day. They have since been going for his outhouses, back-cottages, servants' rooms and W.C.'s time after time in a most merciless manner.

I have never before realized so keenly that I am walking on the brink of the grave. It is really shocking, while still meditating how one of your fellow creatures met his fate at the shell of the Dutch cannon, to hear that many more had their legs and 'sinqes'[31] shattered somewhere; and it is an abominable death to be hacked up by a 94-pounder. People say the reason is that shells being less frequent, the inhabitants are less particular about taking the necessary precautions. I, however, attributed the ludicrous failure of 'Sanna' during the months of October and November to the fact that people were considerably alarmed, and sighed to their creator – of whose possession they were then perfectly certain nearly every second. Their soliloquies were so far retrenched by the perilousness of their position that in their cogitation there was only room for the one word 'God'; and they yearned for the company of his angels more than they cared to meditate sin. But now we have so far forgotten ourselves as to imagine that this failure was•attributable not to providential protection but to Cronje's misfortune and our good luck, or to his cowardice and our valour – what an odd notion.

Friday, 8th
We rose in high spirits preparing for a heavy day's shelling. We wonder whether yesterday's rapid outburst was because they received a fresh supply of ammunition or that Phil-june told them that they had just begun to do damage; but they only hit harder. During the day only an occasional Mauser and about six bangs from their thinner artillery kept us cognizant of the fact that we are beleaguered. What a contrast to unfortunate yesterday.

As a rule the 'Native Question' has, I believe, since the abolition of slavery, always been the gravest question of its day. The present siege has not been an exception to this rule for Natives have always figured pre-eminently in its chief correspondence. The following letter is public property and I have decided on reproducing it[32] *in extenso*:

Mafeking, 8th Dec., 1899.
To General Snyman,
    near Mafeking
Sir, – I beg to thank you for having handed over Lady Sarah Wilson in exchange for the convict P. Viljoen.
    At the same time, I beg to point out that I have only consented to the exchange under protest,[33] as being contrary to the custom of civilized warfare.

In treating this lady as a prisoner-of-war, as well as in various other acts, you have in the present campaign, altered the usual conditions of war. This is a very serious matter; and I do not know whether it has the sanction of General Joubert or not, but I warn you of the consequences.

The war was at first, and would remain, as far as Her Majesty's troops are concerned, a war between one Government and another; but you are making it one of people against people in which women are considered as belligerents. I warn you that the consequence of this may shortly be very serious to your own people, and you yourself will be to blame for anything that may happen.

Regarding your complaint as to your being attacked by Natives I beg to refer you to my letter dated 14th November, addressed to your predecessor, General Cronje. In this letter I went out of my way, as one white man to another, to warn you that the Natives are becoming extremely incensed at your stealing their cattle, and the wanton burning of their kraals; they argued that the war lay only between our two nations, and that the quarrel had nothing to do with themselves, and they had remained neutral in consequence, excepting in the case of the Mafeking Baralongs, who had to defend their homes in consequence of your unjustifiable invasion. Nevertheless, you thought fit to carry on cattle thefts and raids against them, and you are now beginning to feel the consequences; and, as I told you, I could not be responsible. And I fear from what I have just heard by wireless telegraph that the Natives are contemplating further operations should your forces continue to remain within or on the borders of their territories. Before the commencement of the war the High Commissioner issued stringent orders to all Natives that they were to remain quiet and not to take up arms unless their territory were invaded (in which case, of course, they had a perfect right to defend themselves).

Linchwe – of whom you complain – remained neutral until you brought a force into his principal town and looted his traders' stores, and were making preparations for shelling his stadt on the 26th *ultimo*. Having obtained accurate information of these intentions of yours and, warned by what had happened to the Natives near Mafeking, he attacked your laager on the 24th in order to save his town from being shelled and consequent loss of life amongst his women and children. In this I consider he was quite justified, and you have no one but yourself to blame in the matter.

While on the subject of Natives please do not suppose that I am ignorant of what you have been doing with regard to seeking the assistance of armed natives, nor of the use of the Natives by you in the destruction of the railway line south of Mafeking. However, having done my duty in briefly giving you warning on these points, I do not propose to further discuss them by letter.

I have the honour to be,
Sir,
Your obedient servant,
R. S. S. BADEN-POWELL, Col.

'Au Sanna' seems to have been blessed now. The only shot she discharged today did considerable damage. It came at 1.25, just when I was returning from town. It cut across my track and went for the B.S.A. camp in a most sickening whizz. It entered the stable and found several men of the Protectorate Regiment attending their horses; killed one and wounded two. The dead man was singing at the time it went for him.

It is marvellous that while we had 'Sanna's' shells at the rate of 50 per diem, besides hundreds from the thinner artillery, we lost no one; but now nearly every one of her shots kills a man and injures several. I am more keen about my impression of yesterday. People have started football, cricket and polo matches in defiance of shells. The Sunday is a day of gymkhana meetings and merriments which serve as strong counter-attractions to Divine Services. These surely must be one of the causes of the deadliness of the Dutch weapons now. I had entered my pony for a run in next Sunday's races – everybody who knows him was very sanguine that he would take the prize, but I had decided to withdraw him today lest I be guilty of blatant sacrilege and thereby further imperil my dangerous condition. Fancy, only one shot being fired during a very quiet day and carrying off three persons by a single stroke.

Saturday, 9th

Too little, if anything, has been said in praise of the part played by that gallant Britisher – the Barolong herdboy. Cattle are now grazing on what may be termed 'disputed' territory, just where the Dutch and English volleys cross each other; and it is touching to see how piccaninnies watch their flocks, and how in the bright sunshine along the wide plain south and west of the stadt – especially when after filling his belly with a lunch of black coffee and beef – the Dutch artillerist would turn his attention to them, and sate his iniquitous whims by sending a shell right in the midst of a group of them. God would guide it flying over their little heads and it would kindle a mortal fire near them: it is an imposing sight to see them each running after a fragment and calmly picking it up. They would quietly mind their stock or drive them home under a severe shell fire with the tenacity of the African in all matters where cattle are concerned. The chappie killed by that shell that struck the hospital last month was turning goats on the rushes at the back of the hospital. The Boers made a small retort within easy range of a Martini south of the stadt. They had intended to snipe the stadt from there, but the stadt folks made it hot for them. Last week a few herds[34] went straight up to it[35] and brought home some tinned beef biltong and two spades.

Two other herds went out last night. They went out as far as Jackal Tree, where they lay down on the grass near the Boer camp, when the enemy were busy outspanning. It was raining at the time and the oxen were tied up to the yokes. They waited until the owners sheltered themselves from the rain, then advanced and successfully loosened four of the oxen without detection. One of the smart thieves led them away by their riems,[36] while his confederate drove their loot behind.

There is a regiment composed of a mixture of Zulu, Shangaan, Tembu and other Transkeian breeds under one McKenzie, styled the Black Watch. These are camped just where the railway passes Bokone.[37] Some of these fellows on sentry duty saw their Barolong brethren advancing with their highly prized but 'nqabile'[38] possession. The party was mad and an eruption, such as nearly started a revolution in the whole place, ensued. Their row was such as could have attracted considerable attention if 'Au Sanna' was not the lawful claimant for our attention. The case was 'sticking up'[39] and the Colonel judged against the Transkeians, as the Barolong could substantiate their claims by the riems they carried in their hands. The Zulu swore that they brought the cattle from the Boer laager. The Colonel gave the Barolong the third ox and as they were abnormally fat animals he bought the others off them.

This cattle theft has put the Boers on the alert. On Thursday I sent out a man to Kimberley for Vere Stent; he and his companion tried to cross along the railway line but they found the country so excellently guarded by the Boers that to get through was an impossibility. They tried to north-west with the same result and they are now planning a scheme for a fresh try tomorrow. The Barolongs had a brush in miniature with the enemy this morning. About 90 Boers were observed a half-mile to the south of the

stadt waiting for our cattle. When the cattle were cleared away
from the stadt range the Boers stormed the herds who, finding it
impossible to drive the cattle, ran home for arms. Uncle Cornelius[40]
happened to be about and he alone managed to keep the Boers
until his bandolier was empty. Just then about 40 men came up
and drove the Boers off. One of our men got a slight wound and
the Boers wounded three cows and a donkey. We only hope we
have given them something in return.

Sunday, 10th

The usual holy holiday. No Mausering. We have not received
any despatch since last week, when we heard of the relief of
Kimberley. The story by our despatch-carrier that the Boer lines
are impassable must be correct and this accounts for our not
receiving any despatches. Some three of our men have been to
the Transvaal to loot cattle. They went out on Friday and slept at a
farmhouse occupied only by poultry. They killed half-a-dozen
fowls and supped on them. They stayed in a hole all day Saturday
and in the evening advanced towards a Boer homestead which
they had been espying during the day. One of them went to
guard the door of the homestead, with his Martini well cocked,
and ready to 'Quma'[41] – directly a Dutchman (or woman) put out
his head – while the others went to empty a kraal of 14 heads of
cattle that were in it. They took every one of them. They brought
us some interesting news. While at the poultry-house they heard
some voices in the dark, which they recognized as those of some
of our Kalaharis[42] in Rietfontein (now Boer territory). These
Kalaharis were from delivering some Dutch letters, at the eastern
laager, and expressed regret at not having met our men prior to
delivering them as they would have handed them over for our
information and let the Boers 'sweat'. These Bakgalagalis reported
having heard at the laager that there was a heavy fight between
Kimberley and some river or other – probably the Vaal – towards
the end of last moon (end of November) in which both sides lost
heavily. The English lost 'vyf honderd' and the Dutch lost 'tien
honderd'.[43] Our friend Mnr Cronje was also there and his commando was scattered in every direction.

The usual gaiety and merriments took place in the afternoon.

There being no danger I took the pony and went out for a ride
around 'disputed territory' and saw the Boers so close that I
nearly felt inclined to go over and have a chat with them as they
were seated on the ridges of their trenches looking at games

played so merrily round our camp with longing eyes; this, however, is a serious crime and I cannot bring trouble upon myself in that manner. They undoubtedly wonder of what stuff we are made, to look so little the worse for this long siege. I wonder whether they have forgotten that while Cape Town and many important colonial towns have been seats of Dutch governments and still wear Dutch names, Mafikeng[44] has since its creation never been cursed by being a Boer laager, despite strenuous endeavours to make it such. It still bears the name given it by Tau's[45] band of Barolong, who came from Lake Ngami in about 1750. They were a peaceful lot of men, yet they plundered everybody who dared interfere with their migration, and earned for themselves the title of 'Baga Rungoana le Bogale'.[46]

To return to our subject: these West Transvaalians ought to remember that Mafeking has always held her own against becoming Dutch and the only Boer who has owned Mafeking was the one who swore by the honour of the king. It is a pleasant day; fair and cloudy, with an occasional shower every now and then.

Monday, 11th

I went to town early this morning to fetch Mr Hamilton to take pictures in our village for *Black and White*,[47] which paper he represents besides the London *Times*. A shell burst while I was at the residency where I always feel comfortable even if the alarm-bells go. It flew overhead and travelled for miles away in a north-westerly direction. I went to Riesle's for Hamilton and the bells rang while he was still preparing. The discomfort I endured can easily be imagined, for Riesle's is a place which I always hurry to pass quickly – even if there is nothing in the wind. It, however, went towards the railway and exploded there. We then left. Mr Briscoe's[48] drift is not the road to travel, being exposed to the eastern Mausers and shells, particularly when one is on horse-back – so we went to cross by the missionaries' foot drift (Lekoko's new dam). While we were in the plain between the town and our village we observed some heavy firing to the south of the stadt: at the foot drift we were met by several women, who said they were nearly all hit by Mauser bullets while routing 'Lichachane'[49] for fuel. They had to come home minus the wood during a hail of bullets, every one of which fortunately missed them.

When we reached Mr Lefenya's house, we showed the pressman

where lives my old uncle,[50] who kept 90 Boers off on Saturday. I had scarcely finished when the old dame came to meet us and informed me that he had just come home wounded. With the prudence and forethought of the European, Mr Hamilton had every requisite with him and after we had dismounted we went in and washed and dressed the wound, which was, however, not very bad – having entered by the left armpit and exited through the fleshy part of the breast, touching no bones. Little Tiego,[51] chief of the younger corps, had one of his left toes slightly tipped off and two other fellows were wounded, each in the leg – none dangerously. This gives one the idea that the Dutch muskets, unlike their artillery, have had their curses taken off, for this is really the Barolong's first casualty since the war broke out. I am afraid they have given the Boers nothing in return, for directly they got a sufficient view of the Boers the latter retreated hurriedly.

We received news that two despatch-runners were trying to come in here on Thursday night but were fired at by Boers. During their run for dear life the despatches got lost and they have now gone back to Kanya. The man Samuel Lefenya, who cheated the Boers at Ganyesa a few days back, was leaving Mafeking with his wife. They were fired at by Boers and he got dangerously hit in the stomach; his wife was shot in the thigh and they were both taken to the laager. The former is not expected to live. The Boers have been seen picking 130 men and horses for the purpose of reinforcing the north. They say the English are so numerous up there that it is feared they will build the line.[52]

The Boers must have thought that we were now eating horses and were surrendering, because of the white flags leaving for all of the trenches round about us. It was Colonel Baden-Powell sending out copies of the accompanying circular[53] to the burghers, as he says it is exclusively for them and not for the officers and colonial rebels. It is a stirring manifesto, at least to me, but I wonder what its effects will be on Boer ears. We had a quiet day. Some rains set in during the forenoon.

NOTICE
TO THE BURGHERS OF THE Z.A.R.[54] AT PRESENT UNDER
ARMS NEAR MAFEKING.

From the officer commanding His Majesty's Forces, Mafeking.

Burghers, I address you in this manner because I have only recently learned how you are being intentionally kept in the dark by your officers and your Government newspapers as to what is really happening in other parts of South Africa.

As officer commanding Her Majesty's troops on this border, I think it right to point out to you clearly the inevitable result of your remaining any longer in arms against Great Britain.

You are all aware that the present war was caused by the invasion of British territory by your forces, and as most of you know, without justifiable reason.

Your leaders do not tell you that so far your forces have met with what is only the advanced guard of the British force, and that circumstances have changed within the past week; the main body of the British is now arriving daily by thousands from England, Canada, India and Australia, and is about to advance through your country. In a few weeks, the South African Republic will be in the hands of the English; no sacrifice of life on your part can stop it. The question now put to yourselves before it is, is this: is it worth while losing your lives in a vain attempt to stop their invasion or to take a town beyond your borders which, if taken, would be of no use to you? (And I may tell you that Mafeking cannot be taken by sitting down and looking at it, for we have ample supplies for several months to come.)

The *Staat Artillery* have done us very little damage, and we are now well protected with forts and mines. Your presence here, or elsewhere, under arms, cannot stop the British advancing into your country.

Your leaders and newspapers are also trying to make you believe that some foreign continental powers are likely to intervene on your behalf against England. This is not in keeping with their pretence that your side is going to be victorious, nor is it in accordance with the facts. The S.A.R. having declared war and taken the offensive, cannot claim intervention on its behalf. And were it not so, the German emperor is at present in England, and fully in sympathy with us; the American Government have warned others of their intervention on the side of England should any other nation interfere; France has large interests in the gold fields identical with those of England; and Italy is entirely in accord with us; and Russia sees no cause to interfere.

Your leaders have caused the destruction of farms in this country and have fired on women and children, and our men are becoming hard to retrain in consequence. Your leaders have also caused invasion of Kaffir territory, and looting of their cattle, and have thus induced them to rise, and in their turn to invade your country, and to kill your burghers. As one white man to another, I warned General Cronje on the 14th November that this would occur, and yesterday I heard that more Kaffirs are rising, and are contemplating similar moves; and I have warned Snyman accordingly. Thus great

bloodshed and destruction of farms threaten you on all sides, and I
wish to offer you a chance of avoiding it. To this end my advice to
you is to return without delay to your homes and there remain
peacefully until the war is over. Those of you who do this before the
14th instant will be as far as possible protected, as regards yourselves, your families, and property, from confiscations, lootings,
and other penalites to which those who remain under arms may be
subjected when invasion takes place.

Our secret agents will communicate to me the names of those
who do and of those who do not avail themselves, before the 13th
instant, of the terms now being offered.

To ensure their property being respected, all the men of a family
must be present at home when the troops arrive and be prepared to
hand over a rifle and 150 rounds of ammunition each.

The above terms do not apply to officers or to members of the
Staats Artillery, who may surrender as prisoners-of-war at any time;
nor do they apply to rebels from British territory or others against
whom there may be other charges. It is probable that my force will
shortly take the offensive.

To those who, after this warning, defer their submission till too
late, I can offer no promise, and they will only have themselves to
blame for any injury or loss of property that they or their families
may afterwards suffer.

(Sgd.) R. S. S. BADEN-POWELL,
Colonel.

Mafeking, 10th December, 1899.

Tuesday, 12th

'Sanna' never moved till 5 p.m. when she sent five shells into
the location. The thinner artillery and Mausers were very mild.

We had a civil court today. A lot of boys of the firm of Julius
Weil are suing their employers for wages. Mr Spencer Minchin,
LL.B., solicitor (now Lieutenant Minchin, Bechuanaland Rifles),
appeared for all the plaintiffs, and Mr J. W. de Kock, attorney
(now member of the Town Guard), appeared for the defence. It
was a novel court: only the parties concerned looked as usual, but
not the court. The plaintiffs' attorney was in military attire;
lawyer for the defence, never shaved since the siege, all hairy and
dressed in a third-hand suit without a collar, looked more like a
farmer than an attorney. Myself in knickerbockers and without a
jacket, looked more like a member of the football team or a village
cyclist then a court interpreter. All of the natives, but one, carried
their cases.

Wednesday, 13th

Boers held a big meeting in the forenoon, all hands attending. They are undoubtedly discussing Colonel Baden-Powell's mani- festo. Anyhow it put a great change in the situation as they are not shooting in the forenoon any more. One good purpose it served is that they sent a newspaper to the Colonel, probably to contradict his statement that their men are kept in the dark.[55] Besides what the Boers wished the Colonel to see in this paper (*De Volksstem*, 7th December) it contained an account of a big fight at Modder River, in which Cronje, supported by some Free State commandos, made a gallant stand against Lord Methuen.[56] The English, it says, had the worst of it as they had to advance in the open towards a well-fortified opponent. They weakened the south flank and crossed the river and the Free Staters retired. Cronje held his fire well and was compelled to retire by the retreat of the Free Staters, who left their dead on the field and fled to Jacobsdal on the road to Bloemfontein. This is an excellent entertainment considering the long time we remained without news.

Thursday, 14th

'Sanna' was quiet all the morning and commenced duty in the afternoon. The first shot made straight for Sibale's house. It was full of people – women and children – including 'uninikazi', [57] Mrs P. Sidzumo. It pulled and shook the whole house upon them: pieces of shell or the house cut off her toes, shattered her legs and injured her face and head. The left leg was broken below the knee (and the thigh completely shattered). The other people remained alive in the debris. The poor husband, coming to see the remains of his house, was met with the ruins of his wife just pulled out of the debris. He became so senseless that he returned to the fort hardly knowing what he was doing until they told him that his wife wanted to see him. He jumped up in joyous bewilderment – for he had first imagined that she was dead already – and had a look at her before she was moved to the hospital. This was 3.45 and she died at 6.00 in the evening, leaving the husband and a little girl to mourn her loss.

We are very hard up for news. More despatch-runners went out last night but returned to say they found the Boer lines impassable. We had always received two despatches every week. Now we have not received any for ten days and we really feel the strain.

Friday, 15th

Mrs P. Sidzumo was buried at 3 o'clock this morning. She had been in the stadt yesterday afternoon and her husband came to call her back to the scene of yesterday's disaster.[58] They went to the location together. When her husband proceeded to the trench she remained at her ill-fated home, and waited unconcernedly for the hour of this sudden tragedy. The little girl is not cognizant of her bereavement and plays about well at her granny's place.

There was a fight at the Natal border in which General Joubert's forces were completely disorganized and large numbers of them killed, General Joubert himself being taken prisoner.

We have heretofore received nearly all our news by telegraph, from the Boer laager, whence it was conveyed by our people into Mafeking.[59] Mistakes have, of course, been made with regard to names, locations and numbers of casualties, but they may be excused on that score as they are no mathematicians or scholars of any kind. Now even if Joubert himself is not caught we will say that it is somebody and that it is some very important personage whose arrival deserves considerable fuss in the Transvaal.

Even the *Mafeking Mail*, which regards the Native as a mere creature, was this day wont to say: 'Although the following statements from Native sources may only be rumour retailed, so many of the reports brought to hand through similar intelligence have been corroborated by official report received some weeks later, that we feel disposed to give more credence to a Kaffir *ipse dixit* than we formerly have done.'[60]

Anyhow if official intelligence is to be relied upon there were, at the end of last month, 10 000 troops in Ladysmith and General Buller was advancing with 25 000 more. If truth is not stranger than fiction, what then prevents such large armies from catching the old general?[61]

I cannot make out why we are not getting any despatches, for we have people other than letter-carriers going out and coming in. There must be something radically wrong in it.

Monday, 18th

This has been an exceptionally quiet day. 'Au Sanna' never moved at all. Only the thinner artillery and a few Mausers 'shook the dust off their feet' a little. This is the first siege holiday 'Sanna' gave us since her debut on the 23rd October – about 3 months ago.

We received some news on Sunday but still we would not object to more, particularly since what we received was not in black and white. The 'liar' had a very interesting item[62] to cheer us up, but as we could test the authenticity of this with our field-glasses, we instantly flung it back in his face with thanks.

Two fellows were seen on disputed territory this morning. They were arrested and pleaded that they had left but last night in order to 'hamba inkomo',[63] which job they had found too tough. They saw, they said, seven loaded wagons leaving 'Sanna's' fort for Johannesburg during the night. One of the wagons contained 'Sanna' drawn by 16 mules, minus her legs (two wheels) which were drawn by 12 mules. They are not expert liars as they would not have said that the big gun has only two wheels; still, a good many whites and the majority of our people disbelieved our field-glasses in favour of these lies for 'Au Sanna' did not discharge a single shot all day today.

Tuesday, 19th

Early this morning we were aroused by the sound of big guns to the west, north, east and south-east. They were the English molesting the Boers, who have heretofore been having things all their own way. The occasional tapping of the Maxims entertained us with that sweet music I have already described, and we enjoyed it advantageously.

The English are among the foremost warriors of their day. Here we have only a few soldiers representing the wisdom of their nation in a most demonstrative manner. They not only invent miracles but know how to utilize them at random, under thunder and lightning, through all circumstances.

The large number representing our supply of 'Sanna' for today have only been fired about sunrise in an endeavour to smash up the little English boys, who dare poke their fingers in Big Ben's eye. They are only within a stone's throw of this big gun, but it failed to hit them as not a single Dutchman can see them. They can only see the smoke emanating from the naked ground. The Barolongs who fought Snyman and Cronje under Montshioa, many years ago, freely admit that if at their time the Boers brought something half the size of 'Sanna' to bear on them, they would have started a mutiny if Montshioa had refused to hoist the white flag after it burst two shells in their village; but today, through the wisdom of the Englishman, 'Sanna' is regarded

merely as a member of the siege community, also entitled to earn
a livelihood.

I have not mentioned that when a shell was not well charged it
does not explode when it reaches its destination. People pick
them up and sell them; and townsfolk paid for them as follows:

1-pounder Maxim shell	@	£ 10–6
The new 5-pounder	@	£2– 2–0
A 7-pounder	@	£ 15–0
'Au Sanna'	@	£6– 6–0

Prices are on the ascent as shells are becoming rare. ('Sanna'
formerly sold at £3–0–0.) Yet even if 'Sanna' does explode people
do get money for her fragments. The base only fetches 10/6d and
the numerous fragments may bring the total for one explosion up
to two guineas. These shells are therefore a boon in one sense.

Wednesday, 20th

Monday was the hottest day we have had since the siege, but
yesterday was the worst. The heat was intense. Mrs Molema had
to clear to the hut for the night with the children, as the house
was becoming an oven.[64] I tried to stay and fight it out but was
compelled to leave the house to sleep outside at about 11 p.m. I
went to sleep in the lea of the house, which I found was as
convenient as a garden in the afternoon. I slept soundly until
woken by a chilly breeze at 1 a.m. – a marvel of a change for two
hours, surely. I felt quite seedy the moment I packed up to turn in
again. I knew that it had done me a lot of harm for I had a dazy
light head at the time, which caused me to feel very uncomfortable
– as I have never felt any sort of pain during the siege. In the
morning I was not able to get up, and I was in bed all day.

Early this morning someone came to tell us that Meko's pretty
little daughter had breathed her last and so did old Setuki, an
important personage among the Lekomas.[65]

Mausering very mild. Our big guns startled the Boers this
morning but the latter made no response. They went for them
again this afternoon and a few shots were exchanged. Since
Dingaan's Day,[66] Big Ben has had so much to do directly under
his nose, that he has no time to be firing at the homes of women
and children and sick people.

Thursday, 21st

I have not been able to turn out. I hear that a thief has been sentenced to death today by the Court of Summary Jurisdiction. The C.S.O.[67] will of course have to review the case before the sentence is executed.

At 6 p.m. 'Sanna' discharged a sharp shell burst in town with extraordinary force. I hear it has once more gone for the ruins of the Mafeking Hotel. I wonder what Mr Riesle did to those Boers?

We feel the strain very much. It is seventeen days since last we had news. If things go on in this way I wonder what our lot is going to be.

Friday, 22nd

A quiet morning. Not yet able to get up. It is influenza that I have got.

I hear that two Bangwaketse have been out to loot. They managed to lift some sheep in their choice selection but when they were nearly across the Boer lines during the smaller hours of the morning, one of these sheep commenced to bleat. This put two Boers on their track. What a pity that the two Bangwaketse were not armed as the Boers would presumably not have dreamt to venture near them. The Boers fired several shots at them but with the extraordinary tenacity of the Bechuana in all matters where stock is concerned, one of them preferred to stay with their treasure when the other ran away. The latter came 'to tell the tale'. He says his mate is either killed, caught or wounded. The former is the most probable of the three as they fired very vehemently after our informant took to his heels.

David is really 'wa limala'.[68] Last week he was riding Mr Molema's stallion and it tripped and fell, and both horse and rider were wounded. When he got up with his right side all bruised he found that the saddle had been neatly placed to the east of him, with the girths cut to pieces; the horse was standing a little to the west, bleeding on the knee and forehead. This afternoon he rode to town on my pony – one of the best riding horses in the place. He only got as far as the railway line when the pony tripped and chucked him over his shoulders and a serious accident took place. His left side (the one that escaped in the stallion incident), and that of the horse, were injured. The bit of my new bridle got twisted 'uit de fatsoen',[69] and [there were] other wrongs and injuries.

I am inclined to attribute it to reckless inattention rather than 'bad luck', as he calls it, for the first time he returned just at the brink of the grave through a similar mishap, and two falls from the best chargers in the country within a week beats creation. Besides we have not been sitting still, and why did we not knock blood out of ourselves and horses, sides, faces, knees, jaws and do other damage [like he did]?

Saturday, 23rd

An official publication announced that tomorrow will be our Christmas as we cannot depend on the enemy giving us holiday on Monday. So this is our Christmas Eve. A lovely morning, fair and cloudy, giving us a quiet and enjoyable atmosphere. Best of all we have received news after 19 days. It is a lot of news – by private people who of course inform us of the doings of our enemy around us, and bring gossip from the enemy's camp (where newspapers and letters arrive as regularly as ever) – about the occurrences and progress of the war all round the Transvaal, of very recent dates.[70]

Sunday, 24th

Christmas Day. I am not yet able to turn out but I hear that a good many people are going to keep it up as high as is practicable.

I remember my low state with an afflicted sense. To think that this is the second Christmas of my wedded life and I have to spend it, like the first one, so very, very far away from the one I love above all: it is becoming too big and I wish I could drive the thought from my mind. Still, I remember last year[71] when I spent three lengthy, solitary days in old Ma-Diamond's[72] beautiful garden and she fed me with the first issues of her fructuous grove in fruits and greeneries. I told her how happy we would both be if my kind little wife, whom she very much longed to see, was with us; we were consoled, however, by the knowledge that she was on that day presenting my first-born to his saviour under a magnificent Christmas tree somewhere, and that she would sooner or later bring us our little darling boy who would positively be the happiness of our hearts next Christmas (today) in the same garden, the cultivation of our aged lady friend. But here I am today so very far from having that expectation of our calming meditations fulfilled. I am not even graced with as little as a congratulatory missive from both of them, but am nailed to a sick-bed with very poor attention – worst of all, surrounded by Boers. I had expected a ready-dressed chicken from my friend Meko as I have developed a dire hatred for all other food, and (indeed) was almost starving when David came from him with two. Hence I discovered that despite my mental tribulations I was not absolutely friendless. I sent back to them St Leger's cream coloured lappie[73] and 'seo sa ga buti'[74] for their little boy, for which they returned hearty Christmas thanks.

I saw little of the open air but all that reached my ears was full of merriment so there must have been some happy things going on.[75] It was raining somewhat pleasantly all the evening.

Monday, 25th

A really lovely morning after last night's rain. I went to sit on the verandah and drank deeply of the soft balmy air and enjoyed the atmosphere with the sentiments of one watching a classical show of myth and melody. I only thought – but scarcely spoke: everything had brightened up in the most unusual gaiety. Surely we have never had anything like this since the beginning of October; in fact Mafeking never looked so serene all the time I [have] numbered among her inhabitants – and yet I saw Mafeking only as much as was exposed to the eye from the verandah of our house. I have always maintained that no day that the good lord will give us during the siege can in any way equal the ordinary Sunday in beauty – but this excels anything I have yet experienced. I believe that our respected commander, though mindful of the fact that prudence can never be a mistake, sees that there was no occasion to celebrate the Messiah's nativity yesterday instead of on this most beautiful of glorious days.[76] Pretty well-dressed young men roaming up and down the village and happy voices of hundreds of merry girls to the east and to the west made me wish I was able to rise and admire the proceedings.

Lady Sarah Wilson sent down a collection of toys and sweets for distribution amongst the children of our village. Contented little black faces musing over their gifts reminded me of a little fellow far away, who enjoys whatever he gets at the expense of the comfort of a bewildered young mother, deserving a Christmas box from his father but unable to get it. It squeezed out of my eyes a bitter tear – its course is bitter for I have never felt anything like it since the long and awful nights in 1897 when my path to the union that brought about his birth was so rocky.[77]

Surely providence has seldom been so hard on me.

Tuesday, 26th

Early this morning we were aroused by the sound of big guns, muskets and Maxims towards Game Tree. It lasted for nearly an hour, then all was quiet again. It was a good number of the garrison endeavouring to capture a Dutch fort at Game Tree. FitzClarence figured among the ringleaders again and everyone was sure that – bullets failing – he would capture the Dutch fort at the point of the bayonet, but they unfortunately found it a tough business. They got up to the fort and were preparing to jump right into it amongst the Boers. But the walls were so high that only a few managed to get on top. Even here they could do nothing as the trench was too well roofed and the Boers, who meanwhile had their rifles through the loop-holes, played havoc with them until they hoisted the Red Cross. FitzClarence alone got inside and stabbed two or three. They shot him once but he proceeded to bayonet another when they shot a second time and he dropped down – though not dead. (Three who went to the door of the trench were taken prisoners.) He is now in the hospital improving. I think the wounding of FitzClarence incapacitates an eminent 'moguli'[78] from taking part in future operations against the Transvaal, when the troops cross the border. The Boers never hit so hard a blow on Mafeking since they besieged us. Altogether we lost 23 men killed and 26 wounded. The rest of the day was quiet.[79]

Wednesday, 27th

A very quiet and pleasant day, fair and cloudy. I was able to get up this morning and hope to be about soon. Nothing happened during the day. In the evening David entertained me with some Lenkoaniacs,[80] which I enjoyed very much. He once found Hyena Jones covered with a thick blanket in his room in the daytime. David's lips were just about to part when he hushed him in a faint voice and informed him that his time was extremely short – so short that the devil already knew with how many nitches of the tape-measure it will 'lingaana'.[81] I presume it is to be inferred from this that Jones' soul will go to the devil when it departs this life. David, however, took to himself the liberty of putting to him certain abridged interrogations concerning his ailment in the most sympathetic manner, and to his surprise every one of his queries made Hyena 'weller'.[82] He was travelling so accurately, though slowly, along the path of recovery that he was eventually able to remove the thick blanket off his body with the extraordinary remark that his respect for David was as great as his astonishment at his piousness. For David was among the very rare specimens of Christianity on the face of the globe able to cure a dying person simply by motion of their lips; and he stood up and started tidying the room with his usual healthy and civilized way of doing things.

Besides a lot more he [David] told me how Hyena once determined to settle the love question with his rival with a thing a little more deadly than his tongue – for which purpose he procured a rifle. He took a companion with him and bragged as they went along – but he forgot to shoulder the rifle, and took to his heels immediately the rival put in an appearance. On one occasion (shortly after his arrival) Jones nearly assaulted him for having told an enquirer that Mrs Lenkoane was at work, instead of which she had gone out for a walk – he told some such lie. 'Mma, ke tseba bora ba batho ba jwale ka bo Phooko. When ach yue khoing to atopt the wase of sophilised people? Ke sa tsua chata hona jwale. What will the chentleman think of me to hear that my wife is at work?'[83]

Our Civil Commissioner is a white Lenkoane. His acumen in fixing sarcastic phrases and aptitude in putting comical jokes is beyond description. His mere silence gives him a very ferocious appearance.

On Sunday he sent word to all hands that his servants – he had about a dozen of them – should all turn up on Monday to a grand Christmas dinner he was going to give them. They rolled up en masse, but were surprised to find everything in much the same manner as when the pudding party in no. III *Royal Reader* got some pudding[84] – except that these poor fellows received not even the aroma of a grand Christmas dinner. The officers came for their meal at the usual hour, and when they departed the ole buck[85] quickly retired to his bomb-proof for his after-lunch siesta – leaving the disappointed menials to take their way, with dismay written on their faces in bold letters. This is Wednesday already, and he has not yet offered them the slightest excuse for the inopportune treatment.

Thursday, 28th

It is raining very much. Two runners came in from the south this morning. Everybody is full to overflowing, the news they brought being too sweet and too much for the capacity of the human stomach. They bring news of two victories by our relief party – one at Fourteen Streams and one at Phokwane.[86] The former was on the 18th. As Lady Sarah Wilson came here on the

7th and heard in the Boer laar that Lord Methuen had arrived in Kimberley, we have expected this for a very long time.

I am afraid someone's stomach will burst – so nice is the news. Mr Molema last night brought me a copy of the *Bulawayo Chronicle*, from Captain Marsh. It was dated the 2nd instant, a very early date for any newspaper. Every paper unfortunate enough to find its way into Kimberley must pass through so many hands that when one comes across it it is quite worn out and requires to be handled with the greatest care. It contained two accounts of Lord Methuen's fighting at Belmont[87] against Free State burghers. One account was the Dutch general's reports to Oom Paul[88] on the same fight, reproduced from the *Standard and Diggers' News*. The other was the British report, on the same affair, received by an official despatch from Cape Town.

Report No. I says: I had a heavy fight all day against the British troops under General Buller and killed no fewer than two thousand (2 000) of them; commandant some-one-or-other was wounded in the arm but not before he inflicted serious losses on them. The burghers stuck to their ground well, but were compelled to retreat by the overwhelming number of the English who covered five miles of ground. There were 7 000 of them against 1 400 burghers. They had 24 cannons and we had only four.

It is impossible to give the number of our losses. Still it is not great.

Report No. II was pert and pithy: we drove them from one kopje[89] to the other in each of which they had strong fortification. From the last we repulsed them with four guns posted on the opposite kopje and they retired so hurriedly they did not stop to take shelter in the laager. We destroyed the laager, 50 000 rounds of rifle ammunition and 300 shells. Altogether we took 40 prisoners and buried 20 dead Boers. We lost 58 officers and men killed, and 151 wounded.

I suppose the local general reported on Tuesday about Game Tree that he fought the whole of Mafeking garrison with a stray scrap of his commando and killed 600 British – half of the garrison. This discrepancy is something like a report of the fight on the Natal side of the border, in which a Boer commandant, infuriated by the British, says there were 10 000 British troops against 800 Boers, only 400 of whom were fighting.[90]

Friday, 29th
The rain stopped for a while last night and started again this

morning. It continued all day today. Mausering was consequently very mild. Only 'Sanna' went very hot today.

I was able to turn out this morning and found many people in town down with the sickness I had – it's influenza. I returned from town just in time, for the rains started two minutes before I reached home. I did some interpreting for half the Dutch women-folk of the women's laager in a very long case in court. It was the only one, but kept me busy for a longer period than the usual session when ten or fourteen cases are on the roll. It was a charge against a Dutch damsel, a member of a local well-known family, of having stolen £90–12–0, the property of a lady of the same nationality. Both complainant and accused are domiciled in the women's laager and the former carried this money about her, as it would have been commandeered if she took it to the Standard Bank.[91] The mode of living in the women's laager is so shabby that there was no safer place for the money than her hand-bag, and that is how the unfortunate girl got access to it. They are a family of 'mahlwembu'[92] who had severally been under pecuniary embarrassments. Her lavish purchases and repeated acts of generosity laid the robbery bare. The prisoner pleaded not guilty. The case is remanded till tomorrow – Saturday the 30th.

The Game Tree fiasco appears to have been a heart-rending burlesque. Never was such a wilful suicide committed by a community in our condition. The Colonel Commanding – it appears – was forced into permission of the thing against his will. He recently wanted the Barolong to go and capture the cattle from the Western Boer laar. But Lekoko[93] gave him such reasonable reasons that he convinced him to the belief that everyone would be killed before seeing the cattle, and all the heart in him dwindled away; he[94] was bound to believe that the greatest and most prominent way of proving our bravery would be by sitting quietly and defending our place until the arrival of the troops.[95]

He[96] also went half-way with them and at dawn they advanced towards the place, walking along in broad daylight, the Boers having their rifles cocked through the loopholes just waiting for them to approach. It is a marvellous thing that they were not all killed, for it was a regular self-murder, as they had no cover whatever. The Boers waited until they were within a hundred yards – then loosed a hail of bullets among them. The officers took the lead and skipped towards the 'armoured trench' – every one of the men following. They jumped on top with the intention of using the bayonets, but found the place too well-roofed for the purpose. The Boers were meanwhile playing havoc with the others who were then endeavouring to shoot them through their own loop-holes. They were already without officers when they reached the fort. Some had revolvers even through the loop-holes, and one held the barrel of a Mauser on the outside and stuck his bayonet past it. It was a lamentable affair and the least said about it the better. The consternation amongst the inhabitants was so deeply rooted that it is clearly visible amongst men and women and old and young of both whites and blacks.

Saturday, 30th

A West African,[97] giving evidence in a city police court, once described the cause of the proceedings as 'a h-ll of a smash', but I believe a real 'h-ll of a smash' was the wreck of the charge office by 'Sanna' this morn. Such a destruction of the charge office is really a narrow shave for the court house. Many or all of the prominent places like Whiteley's, Weil's, Dixon's, the bank, the neat little rondavel of the market hut, etc., have all taken their turns in the test of 'Sanna's' dexterity, but the court house, much to the extreme disgust of the inhabitants who, seeing 'Sanna's' agility at wrecking buildings, imagined that, it being the head official building, it was their chance of getting the new court they have so long been agitating for. I believe it's saved intentionally by the Boers, for the residency also, and the gaol, have never been hit. Turning to our subject, the ruin of the charge office was just as lamentable as many of 'Sanna's' doings, and it was also the occasion of a marvellous escapade. It entered, and shook down the office. It found 50 Natives, who had taken shelter in front of the ill-fated building when the tocsins[98] chimed. The many fragments found their way away from the presence of human beings and only singled out a good young fellow (one of the Maseloas),[99] threw the top of his head away from his body, and left him standing exactly where he was: all this was the work of a second – or a lesser period. Every one of his companions spent a long time reflecting over the narrowness of his own escape. Sheets, half sheets and fragments of corrugated iron were scattered all over the street, and they did not notice the occurrence till many minutes after.

A deserted young Zulu from the Boers reports that at the unfortunate burlesque, the fiasco at Game Tree on Tuesday morning, ten Boers were killed and ten wounded. They say it was

Jameson who attacked them.[100] Miss Bezuidenhout's case[101] has not yet been decided: it is further remanded until Tuesday.

Young Maseloa was buried in their kraal today.

Sunday, 31st

Ou-Jaarsdag.[102] The usual thing. No thunder and no danger. The Colonel and Civil Commissioner were down to settle an issue among the Chiefs. The cause of the trouble was of course – Thelesho.[103]

With Sidzumo, Nyangi[104] and Miss Moloza, in the afternoon I went to have a close scrutiny of my Dutch friends across the disputed territory.

We called in at 7 p.m. He[105] was half-way at his cups and had a great many objections to make. He wondered why the authorities, seeing that the whites are afraid of the Boers, don't arm the Barolong, as they would certainly go and rifle the 'God-damned brutes away'. And also, why the issue of grain has since this morning been so regulated that no one is allowed to buy more than 6d worth at a time.

The former[106] would cause us to run over to the enemy and ask him for permission to settle outside peacefully and plough as usual, while the latter would evoke such a mutiny in camp as would put an end to the siege – which wouldn't be existing at the end of next week. He also set us giggling by informing us how Wessels habitually parts with his £50 after receiving his quarterly allowance. He would send several Cape Boys to buy some brandy for him. He would keep on sending one after the other and the last two or three would depart when the first had already returned, after which the old fellah would be so miserably under the exuberance of the damning drink as not to recognize the rest of them. Each of them would then pocket the 3/- and not bother about buying the brandy at all.

The process would be just the same with others whose role it was to visit the butcher, baker, grocer etc. The messages would be duplicated, triplicated and even quadruplicated, and as the necessary money would be furnished on each occasion they would all stand by quietly and wait for the first Cape Boy, then safely convert the money to their own use, without fear of any judicial proceedings.

EDITORIAL NOTE

The nature of the siege changed unmistakably in December, and this month set the tone for things to come. The Boers did not attack during the period, though rumour had it that one offensive was cancelled at the last moment. Thus, apart from the Game Tree incident, confrontation was restricted to artillery bombardment, sniping and brief skirmishes.

The two internal enemies faced by the besieged populace, however, began to make themselves felt: accidents through the detonation of unexploded shells accounted for life and limb, and boredom became a creeping paralysis that demanded an antidote. Diversionary activity, aimed at distracting and amusing the citizenry of Mafeking, was planned in an attempt to alleviate this discomfort. Sundays saw the organization of gymkhanas, polo matches and other sports in which soldiers and civilians participated enthusiastically. Baden-Powell himself took a leading role: apart from playing polo, he arranged satirical pageantry – in which he appeared as a ludicrously overdressed ringmaster – in order to boost morale. The *Mafeking Mail* also injected a measure of fun into this by printing results and, more often than not, lively comment. Also, Sunday-night concerts were presented. A music ensemble entertained audiences with more serious items while Baden-Powell and any others who could be recruited provided musical and satirical sketches. This revelry – which depended for its success on Boer recognition of the Sunday truce – no doubt relieved the pressure on the besieged population. Perhaps this is one reason why the Africans of *Mafikeng*, who had little part in the diversionary activities, were later to feel the pressure to a far greater extent than their allies across the railway line.

Although these programmes broke the monotony with weekly regularity, Christmas was a singular occasion. The townsfolk – with the energetic help of Ben Weil – ate festive dinners, either at the hotels (which provided surprisingly sumptuous repasts, when it is considered that rationing was soon to be imposed) or in shell-damaged homes. Morale was high – especially as a result of the 'double' Christmas brought about by the unique situation. But this was to ebb the very next day with the Game Tree disaster.

On the Boer side of the line of investment a general 'tightening-up' was being put into effect. Hence, while little attempt was made to enter the town, the besieging forces ensured that it would not be easy to leave it. Their success is measured by the fact that cattle-raiders, despatch-runners and spies found it increasingly difficult to pass through the lines. One might have expected that Baden-Powell's proclamation of 10 December would have been followed by an escalation in their offensive; but this never occurred. Instead the Boers sat tight and permitted the hardships of the besieged to take their course.

In fact, few physical difficulties had yet been faced. In town there was still an adequate supply of food, and the citizenry were becoming accustomed to the regular explosion of shells. The picture in the *stadt*, where shelling accounted for more lives, was not quite as optimistic – yet it was far from serious. True, grazing had become scarce (although frequent rains ameliorated this situation too). But the Barolong were still far from eating the dog-flesh that became a substantial part of their diet later on.

CHAPTER 3

January 1900

Monday, 1st

The first day of the first week of the first month in 1900. Not at all a lovely morning. The distant pop of the Mauser distinctly shows that there is no holiday for poor beleaguered us. I tried to go to town but 'Au Sanna', going strong, caused me to come back and take shelter. I wonder why some people call her 'Grietje', as 'Griet'[1] for a thing of her potency would be nearer the mark. She was exceptionally 'kwaai' all day today. Goodness knows what provoked her.

After I went to town and David and Ebie[2] were breaking-fast the thing smashed within 50 yards from the house. David cleared helter-skelter with the coffee which had become insipid. Ebie considered his bread too precious and remained chewing as if nothing had happened. In the afternoon things were very warm. I have developed a nasty fear for 'Sanna'. She has, since Dingaan's Day, devoted her time to our little gun across the river, and we have now become unused to her. I wonder why she is so hot today.

In the afternoon David stood watching a train of merry girls, amidst whom were Meko's sisters-in-law in the best of millineries, celebrating the new year with several jolly games. All of a sudden 'Sanna' came round and spoiled the whole thing. Mr Briscoe's garden is an intolerably near spot for 94 pounds of mortar to burst while a train of giggling girls are enjoying the first day in the first year of the twentieth century near Bokone – particularly when they were under the impression that it was directed to town. It sent nearly all the merry maidens in different directions. Some lay flat on the ground – it was for dear life – and 'Sanna' fairly put them in memory that their lives were dearer and more expensive than their new year's dresses.

One shell burst near Weil's this morning. The employers had a narrow escape and two mules which happened to be about were killed on the spot. One burst near the commissariat yard. A fragment came in contact with one of the labourers and eviscerated him which, in short, means killed him on the spot. A few broken walls completed the total for today. 'Sanna' was very hot today, and so was a beastly new 7-pounder to the east of the town which at one time caused me to leave the Market Square post-haste – it was for dear life.

Tuesday, 2nd

The 7-pounder that fired from the east yesterday had been moved round to Jackal Tree during the night. It sent a number of shells into the stadt early this morning, one of which smashed inside the hut of Mma-Mokoloi and emptied its contents on her head. None of the others were injured. The baby at her breast was not even shaken. A shell from 'Sanna' hit the east of the stadt, where Ellitson has put up his slaughter-pole since the siege,[3] and amputated an employee in a most piteous manner – both legs and both arms. He died after this.

Wednesday, 3rd

It was not the 7-pounders which killed Rra-Mokoloi's wife, but a 12-pounder. Opinions differ on the point and some call it 9-pounder; however, its shells are said to be far more dangerous than any yet used by the enemy on Mafeking. It is posted somewhere west of the stadt.

They have turned their attention away from the Rooi-neks[4] and have decided to knock spots out of the 'verdomde[5] Kaffers' this morning. They are shelling the stadt from east and west. There is a miscellaneous collection of Natives from Johannesburg who thought that the war would last a month or less. They came here as they thought Mafeking was safe enough to spend the month, after which they would return to the revolutionized Rand. They are a miscellaneous collection and include Pondos, Shangaans, Barotse, Zambezian and South Central African breeds. They are harmless lot of people – some of them live under the two trees on the space between the B.S.A. Police camp and the stadt. They do a little night's toil when they require a little cash to buy grain which they 'nona'[6] with horseflesh. They are quiet and are waiting for the end of this trouble, and I am sure they would not do any harm to anybody.

This morning I was trying to go to town. I was just near the two trees when the bells rang. There was a horrible smash all round me and I could see the branches of one of the trees flying in the air in a cloud of dust. From under the tree all the men in the

shade were raised from four to seven foot high. After the smash I
thought that thunder seldom strikes twice the same place, and I
pressed my nerves to see how my fellow creatures had been
jumped upon by this meanest part of the scum of the German
race. But the good lord's potency is marvellously demonstrative
when he wishes to frustrate the termination of a wicked man. His
good angels had preceded the shell, shifted the men apart, and
made a way for it. It burst amongst them in a most indescribable
awfulness, but not one of them was hurt. There was a furrow
where it ploughed the ground among their bedding. The camel-
thorn tree suffered fearfully, but not one of the men got a single
scratch. However, I was filled with fear and I turned back to take
shelter. I had hardly reached the Meko's when there was another
terrific smash. It burst five yards from them; this time the
fragment flew over their heads but injured nobody.

Things were a bit quiet about dinner time. The 12-pounder
was meanwhile circuiting back to the east. It took up its position,
apparently to resume operations in the afternoon, but they had
hardly time to digest their lunch of black coffee and ox meat
when Baden-Powell's chappies showed them that they had something nasty for Boer flesh in store in Mafeking. Three 7-pounders,
posted within range of the big gun last night, and a little
Nordenfeld started to boom one by one. Their shells raised
clouds of dust as they demolished the earth-works which form
the Boers' entrenchments. The little Nordenfeld is a very great
friend of 'Sanna's' – we'll call it 'three-pounder'. It and 'Sanna'
always had duels resulting in very little success for either side,
just like a fight between two bulls of the same age. Three pounds
against ninety-four – can anything be funnier? Now just imagine
the former being reinforced by three times seven and you have
an idea of the duels that ensued. People who in the morning
were frightened out of their wits had an opportunity of turning
out and watching the artillery duel. The state artillery with
proper soldiers directly under their nose had no time to think of
shelling a town full of unarmed people, and we walked about as
freely as if we were in Cape Town, for they warmed up the Boers
until about dusk.

While she was in the west this morning, the 12-pounder
managed to kill a volunteer in the White fort.[7] Whilst they were
beckoning the stretchers with a Red Cross flag the gun sent three
shells into the women's laager. A fragment of the first killed a
child of Mrs Erasmus, prosecutrix in the *Regina versus Emily*

Bezuidenhout theft of £90, and wounded a little boy so fearfully that he is not expected to live.

Ma-Mokoloi died today in hospital. This has been an unfortunate day for both man and beast. Two horses were wounded in town, three cows and a goat killed near the stadt, and Mr Bell's cow received a Mauser bullet in her neck. Poor dame! This is the second Mauser on the neck since the siege.

Another shell burst in the south; we wonder how long this is going to last. Instead of getting brighter, the prospect in front of us is darkening itself. I am inclined to believe that the Boers have fully justified their bragging, for we are citizens of a town of subjects of the richest and the strongest empire on earth and the burghers of a small state have successfully besieged us for three months – and we are not even able to tell how far off our relief is. It is certain that it cannot be too near. As the last despatches told us that the Boers were at Stromberg, Cape Colony and as far down as Estcourt in Natal, this is a capital stroke and fully justified their bragging. It is a shame on the part of the Imperial Government to 'kgotla semane'[8] before they have tested their abilities to face it.[9] Now they let us square the account while they lounge on couches in London City, reading their newspapers and smoking their half-crown (2/6) cigars. It is a difficult thing to maintain a bright face when so many are ruining young cheer. In the month of October the British had been victorious against the Boers – so victorious that we were under the impression that the Natal chaps will line the border from the 1st of November. Instead of that being the case, the Boers have since beleaguered Ladysmith and gone traversing the British territory to as far down as Estcourt. Their progress had, according to the last despatches, not yet been checked.

Thursday, 4th

A very quiet day. I was a broken reed all yesterday, and a man from Maritzani[10] arrived just in time to pull me together.[11] All of the Boers in the district have rebelled[12] with the sole exception of Mr Vos. The latter, a very kind old Dutchman, was our field-cornet at Maritzani. He had been arrested three times and taken to the laager, and on each occasion swore that he will never take arms against the English, even if they wish to shoot him. They have allowed him to go on each occasion. When my informant left Maritzani, however, he had received his final notice: that if he adheres to his views, all of his stock would be taken and his children sent away to Mafeking. He told me a lot more – that the troops had fought at the Vaal river. They have previously been travelling to and fro between Kimberley and the Vaal. Since the fight the Boers are not able to tell where they are. Letters have been received at Maritzani from the laager – that there is no use in fighting the English. They always wish to clear away, but are still there – only in obedience to orders; and various other interesting items.

What makes me to believe everything he says is that he heard of the Game Tree fiasco on Saturday last week. They told him that there was a fight in Mafeking in which the Boers lost 27 men and, it is believed, the English lost many more.

Friday, 5th

It was raining softly all night, and the result is a fair and lovely morning.

The presiding officer at the trial of the girl Bezuidenhout, his honour Major H. J. Goold-Adams, being indisposed, she was remanded *sine die*.

Poor Ngidi came in for a very rough time. He was before the court yesterday on a charge of being asleep while on sentry duty the previous night, and was sentenced to be dismissed. He appeared again this morning on a charge of failing to hand over a bag of kaffircorn. The sentence of the court: seven days H.L.[13] and the confiscation of the kaffircorn. Hard luck on poor little Alfred.[14] The following is the cause of his trouble: during the month of November the authorities, deeming it expedient in view of the approaching hard times, forbade the sale of grain of any sort by the storekeeper. All grain belonging to storekeeprs was commandeered, and the government had it retailed cheaply – on economic lines – to the public.

For this purpose they have established a grain store in the stadt, one at the location, and Lippman's in town. Early in December orders were issued to private owners as well that they were to state the amount of grain in their possession, as this drain got a grip of us; and it became imperative that all grain should be collected from private people, and everybody be allowed to buy so little as not to have the slightest chance of wasting anything. It is only by dint of a favour that I was allowed to buy a steen brood[15] per diem. Therefore it is criminal to have in your possession any quantity of grain beyond what the regulations permit you to purchase from one of these stores run on economical lines.[16]

Rice, barley, oatmeal, and sugar[17] have also been included and their sale is restricted unless one has an order which regulates the quantity he can purchase in a certain shop to last him a certain period. A common person would be enriched by this arrangement, as cash cannot procure whatever one requires – he being allowed to purchase so much worth and the balance all remaining in his till. But our[18] case is different: the regulation diet is cheap enough as the purchase price is also regulated, but it is too small to keep a decent man alive. One can only increase his diet by various unrestricted luxuries, the prices of which rule higher than the clouds.

From an official's viewpoint, this restriction is a wise policy, as it prevents the decrease of our supplies from passing faster than the days of the siege. To the merchant it is a boon, in as much as it enables him to demand whatever he desires for his unrestricted dainties. It is a curse, however, in that the money is circulated at the expense of the private individual's pocket.[19]

From a Serolong[20] point of view this whole jumble is more annoying than comforting. For this they may be excused, as the arrangement is in the hands of young officers who know as little about Natives and their mode of living as they know about the man on the moon and *his* mode of living.

It came to their notice that some Barolongali[21] were selling kaffir beer the other day. They look upon it as wasting, or if the scale of this luxury was to continue, they were going to make a case against the party and would have, had the Civil Commissioner not been what he is – a white Native.

They do not know that kaffir beer to a common Morolong is 'meat vegetables and tea' rolled into one, and they can subsist entirely on it for a long time. If ever you wish to see the sense of the word economy, observe the kaffir beer by the amount of water poured into the corn to what is yielded. If prohibited, I wonder what is to become of the bachelor, who is a fighting man and soldier and can therefore not brew it for himself, as it is not sold in any of the three.[22]

The collection of grain is now going on in the stadt unlike at the location. There it is carried away[23] by the chiefs. The officers are under the impression that when the chiefs reach a hut they take away the last crumb they find in possession of the owner, who would henceforth survive on what they purchase economically from the store. The store has been shut for the last five days, because when the regulation was struck down to 6*d* a time,

Barolongali told the storeman he could go to H. This was last Sunday. The store has since been shut. I believe the storeman has gone to Hopetown in obedience to the Black Petticoat Ordinance.[24] I presume the truth is that the officers are either under the impression the Barolongs are able to purchase from a closer store, or that they can live a week without – for otherwise I cannot comprehend. This causes me to believe that they liken Barolongs to the man in the moon, who is at his place every time there is a full moon. The full moon is always at night, when the store is closed, and the man in the moon could not possibly come down for any grain; and it is their belief that Barolong can do the same: for while this 'every-morsel-economical-collection' is in progress, the store shows no sign of reopening – God help these poor beleaguered people.

Ebie has a very bad chest. He has had it for the last few days and he shows no sign of improving. His people 'ncoma'[25] his coughing as that which was never heard in the hut before. Most of the children are down with fever. Further, Molema's cattle and many others have the rinderpest. Mafeking[26] has 'setlhabi'[27] – she can hardly breathe. Sickness has formerly not troubled us very much during the siege; sickness was so rare that I have never heard anyone complain of toothache.

With Selabi all the afternoon. He told me of the welfare of my family. If he is not the boldest 'cheat'[28] in Bechuanaland, I owe him an apology.

Since[29] the middle of the last month we have been tasting to see if the Civil Commissioner's grapes are ripe; so far we have only been able to discover that they are sweet, but we cannot yet tell if they are ripe or green. There is, however, no likelihood of this being found out until there are no more grapes to taste!

This morning I went round for another taste. I tried to pick only as much as necessary for tasting, when the whole bunch came down on my hand – rather a heavy weight. It weighed about three pounds, but I was not the fool to replace it, although it was far too much more than I required. In the afternoon I saw the 'baas'[30] filling his little basket and I went round for another 'discovery', viz., what they taste like. Just when I came in, I heard[31] 'Do you know who steals my grapes, Patrick?'[32]

I carried on bravely. 'No, Sir, I don't.'

'Do you know, Plaatje?'

'I am Plaatje.'

'Do you know who always steals my grapes?'

'No.'

'To steal is no answer . . . By Jove! It is you who always steals my grapes. Can't you fellows do without stealing?'[33]

I thought that the next question might be too unpleasant and I tried to modify the flowing tide before it grew worse, so I began:

'I have only been eating ("eating" mind you and not "stealing") those in front of the stable, Sir.'

'I don't see why you should steal them even if they were at the back of the stable, for your father[34] didn't steal any grapes.'

I successfully stemmed the tide when I interpolated:

'Well, my father didn't work for the Magistrate.'

He turned around and went on with his business. He was still smiling when he eventually gave me the sweetest bunch in the garden!

Saturday, 6th

About a dozen or more of the location people have been summonsed to appear before the Court of Summary Jurisdiction on Monday morning next. (They include the Lumata and Mfazi families,[35] and other prominent locationists.) They must answer to a charge of having wrongfully, unlawfully and maliciously neglected to hand over their grain when requested by the authorities to do so. Things are getting serious. Today was very quiet. We had only two shots from 'Sanna' during the day but the smaller fry was brisk – the smaller the brisker – late in the afternoon. At six o'clock there was a perfect fusillade, and Mauser bullets flew, zip-zip-zip, about the town in the same manner as they did in November last. Everyone wondered what was up.

There have been certain smashes[36] in town during this week, and everybody is tired of the siege. I am afraid some people will be too far gone to welcome our relief when it turns up. It rains nearly every day, but softly enough to keep things in good order.

Sunday, 7th

The usual thing; joy, pleasure, merriment, sports, etc. etc. I met Miss Ngono this morning. I had not seen her for a month, and she was so broken-hearted that when I looked at her face I thought it was starvation telling on her constitution – but the following was the cause: her lover was a member of McKenzie's Black Watch. Whilst out sniping he received [a wound] in the head. He appeared to be recovering, but certainly grew worse at the beginning of this week and ultimately died the other night.

The poor girl is simply thrown on her own resources. Rev. F. G. Briscoe left for Cape Town several months ago without paying her that quarter's salary. Mr Peart, of the town Wesleyans, appears to have exchanged the church for a Lee-Metford and the poor girl must see how she can manage it.

Monday, 8th

A very quiet day – fair and cloudy. It rained softly all the afternoon. Cannoning was mild and Mausering nil. A little boy named Phalaetsile escaped from the Boers yesterday. A poor chappie of only about seven years old, he found himself accidentally in the hands of the Boers three Sundays ago. Some volunteers are always moved from one end of the camp to the other, and he was one of the youngsters that always carried their blankets[37] for a sixpence and part of their rations. They were out looking for a similar job about our farthermost redoubts, when he and a companion played into the hands of the Boers. He has since been employed as a herd in the big gun fort. I am afraid we have seldom had so much news, [even] from a fellow five times his age. He really has sympathy for Britain in his little heart. He made an earthen plan of the big gun fort – with sand and pieces of wood showing the position of the tents, wagons, and horses in it, and also the action of the big gun – so cleverly that the Colonel came to study it. He states there were two artillery duels lately. After the first, two Boers were killed and one had his left arm broken; after the second he found five dead Boers, but he cannot state if there were any wounded. He says the chief gunner was shot during last week and knocks about with the crutch. I asked him why he[38] doesn't lay down when he is wounded. He said, 'Kaitse ke ene ba shupetsang fa toropo e sekgotlho e teng.'[39]

He tells a whole lot of interesting items. He states that during last week someone rode from the head laager to say that the English wrote to say that they shouldn't fire at the hospital. On hearing this the gunners fired two shots at the hospital on purpose. Official publication adds that these are the two shots which fell very close to the hospital on the 2nd inst. There is so much about this interesting little boy that I will never forget. The Colonel came round to the residency for the sole purpose of studying his earthen plan of the big gun fort.

Tuesday, 9th

Shelling was very mild. I cannot say if it was in consequence of

the long 'medupe'[40] that rained nearly the whole day. 'Sanna'
didn't fire a single shot today. Some fellow came with three oxen
they lifted from the Boers. They had another row with McKenzie's
Black Watch. McKenzie's Black Watch are nonsensical and their
action is tantamount to doing the enemy more good than harm; it
cannot be said otherwise, for if people are treated harshly on
their arrival no one will care to go for more cattle and the Boers,
of course, would benefit in that case.[41]

It was only when a party of young Barolong, prompted by the
injustice done to them, challenged them with their rifles, that the
Black Watch yielded to their taking the cattle away – but not
before they had wounded two of them (cattle, not Barolongs).

Wednesday, 10th
Things were somewhat quiet today, but Boer fire was somewhat effective. An innocent man was tapping some water out of a
tank when a Mauser bullet entered his body by the neck, coursed
through his inside and exited through his left loin. He was
stooping down at the time, and stood straight and walked about
a little before he was taken to the hospital on a stretcher; and
died about five hours later. I have also heard of a white woman
being killed during the day.

Thursday, 11th and Friday, 12th
These have been very funny days. Boers hammering away at
us in a most extraordinary manner. Goodness knows what provoked them. Three more fellows went out to look for stock.

Saturday, 13th
We woke to find that my wife has a splendid birthday. A very
quiet morning, Mausering conspicuous in its silence. A quiet
and beautiful day – almost no hammering by the big gun; only
the distant puff-puff-puff-puff of the Nordenfeld tells that there
is no rest for the friend and that there is trouble for the foe. Three
fellows, who went out to loot stocks, had come back this morning
with 20 heads of cattle – bit fat elephants.

The Colonel has ruled [in] a new proclamation that every man
in Mafeking with looted cattle should pay the Government the
fourth part of whatever he brought in. He would have nothing to
do with the oxen, however, and is quite right, for surely if that

was the case fewer men would care about going for cattle – and this is calculated to do the enemy more good than harm. Besides, by taking the cattle away from the enemy a man is assisting the authorities – and why should the authorities come round and fine a man for having helped them? It was like ten weddings in the stadt today. Each of the principal 'kgotlas'[42] being supplied with an ox, we had some swagger dinner – roast beef and the rarest vegetables, and various other dainties.

We had arranged for the purchase of a sheep and kaffir beer to be used at Mathlaseloa's redoubt (this is everything to them) in honour of the occasion of the birthday of Lethlaseloakazi.[43] But we only purchased the latter cheap stuff,[44] meat being too plentiful to warrant a farther expenditure on a sheep. So I sat down and looked on, while the bulk stirred themselves. Such rejoicing never took place in the stadt since there was such a thing as rinderpest.[45] My only trouble was now and then to tell a friend that this is my wife's birthday – and that joy is doubled.

P.S. The following shows that there is a very great difference between white and black even in a besieged town: 'Fresh meat rations to be reduced to ¾ lbs from Monday inclusive.' It is a notice by Capt. Ryan, D.A.A.G., to the townites.[46]

Sunday, 14th

The big gun is away from its fort. Many people say it has left us for good, but I am inclined to the belief that they have moved further away as their present position is very dangerous, [being] under a continuous shellfire from our little Nordenfeld. If I was in their place I would have moved it back soon after the first fellow fell, as there is no necessity for losing any life when I can bomb-shell my enemies from a distance far out of their range – as is the case with the big gun. Bets are in circulation that the Boers have taken it away to Pretoria. They, however, didn't remain undecided for a long time, for in the afternoon it was discovered that they had shifted it across the river to a spot about 3½ miles east – alongside the road to Madikwe.[47] I wonder how they will shoot at us in the morning as they cannot get at a quarter of our town from where it is. I hope they will not merely send shells into the place without aiming at anything.

The plenteousness of our pantry since yesterday causes us to keep up a birthday with the Mahlelebes today. That Mr Bell is given half of one ox is sufficient sign that this is not yet the last of it.

Monday, 15th

'Sanna' has been removed from her fort and is shelling from another position near McMullen's.[48] She gave her début on the Madikwe road at noon today. One thing that frightened me very much yesterday was whether it will be sufficiently in sight for them to give us the warning. But the alarm-bells still rang as they used to do: a ring, two strokes, to warn us that she is loaded and that she is pointed to the south of the camp; and six strokes, to the north. Then a lively gentle finale or 'pasop'[49] when we all dodge into our holes. So my alarm is alert.

The first shell went for a hut at the edge of the stadt. It was quite new and strongly built. It blew the wall clean away, scattered the furniture in every direction and made a way for the reeds, thatched roof and poles to come down to the ground as neatly as though the hut was made like that.

Fortunately no one was inside. Fragments flew all over the neighbourhood, but beyond filling some pots of kaffir beer with sand next door, it injured no one.

Tuesday, 16th

'Sanna' is exceptionally [active] nowadays. Her new position is extremely dangerous to both the residency, where I stop most of the day, and the courthouse, where the summary jurisdiction court sits; all shells have their courses almost invariably over the two roofs. When a shell flies about 20 ft. above the roof you imagine that it will graze your hair. It must, therefore, be worse than nasty when one of her shells flies only 20 inches above the roof and smashes next door as one did during the day. In the afternoon it went for the convalescent hospital in the Railway Institute. Fortunately the sick people were in shelters, so besides wounding a waiter who happened to be about, it played havoc with the furniture. This secondary hospital has since been removed to the Victoria Hospital under cover of the Red Cross. Many of the places knocked about today are not within sight of the big gun. They merely plug shells into the place without knowing what they are going for. A spy has been arrested – on Friday. He admitted that he came from the Boers for purposes of spying, and he is now at the gaol awaiting his fate.

Wednesday, 17th

Summary jurisdiction courts are menaced. Shells select the roof of the courthouse for their course exactly at the court hours, and keep smashing the neighbourhood.

Thursday, 18th

Boers are using some marvellous shells just now. Experts say that they are very new and must be made in Johannesburg. I wonder if the gunners who fire them appreciate the idea that they are better and deadlier than the brand 'Made in Germany'. They seldom burst where they first land, but merely plough the ground for a little distance, then pump right up in the air again and start a fresh journey for one or two more miles before they reach their fag end. This afternoon they sent a shell in the direction of the Market Square. It went through the office of the *Mafeking Mail*,[50] frightened the compositors out of their wits, went into D. Webster's next door, and burst just on top of Vere Stent's bomb-proof. A fragment pierced the wall of Dixon's bar, touched up the head of the proprietor a bit, and scattered the bottles all over the floor. This morning another paid an intrusive visit to the other end of the Market Square and thundered into Lippman's store, completely ragging his office and the goods therein. Little Mr Lippman was choked with dust when he came out, and could hardly apprehend the sympathetic expression directed to him by the bystanders. He was only coughing like 'kgomo ea ntaramane'[51] for about fifteen minutes. One piece hurt the arm of a young lady, fortunately not seriously, and the crowd of purchasers escaped unhurt. In the evening they fired two heavy volleys with three-minute intervals between them; the second one was heavier than 'Sanna's' report.

Friday, 19th

They were firing at our labourers last night. A shell burst in the town hall today. The Bechuanaland Rifles stay there, and a few of them were buried in sand and bits of brick. Others came out with slight shock, but fortunately none were hurt. One shell flew over Meko's house, found a small hut in a hollow, touched the grass works of this, then bumped right up in the air [and] passed over the whole of the stadt. [It] passed over the Limestone fort[52] and burst a little way to the west of it.

In the evening, at 9.15, there was a perfect fusillade during which 'Sanna' fired her 'bad-night'. Volleys were fired by the enemy, and kept up incessantly for some time. I believe it was going to last till midnight, had not our 7-pounder in the river bed sent a couple of 'bumps' at their rifle flashes – which partly quenched their metal. Half-a-dozen puff-puffs from our Nordenfeld produced dead silence. I believe it has 'jumped-up' many of them, as the shots were aimed at their rifle flashes, and no 'shut-up' was ever so abrupt.

Saturday, 20th

Shelling-shelling-shelling – the monotony of the day. The Court of Summary Jurisdiction is held on the west of the court-house outside, in consequence. A big shell struck the abdomen of the town's special constable and fractured his private parts in a most pitiful manner. He is, however, expected to pull through. Sterk[53] Morolong.

Sunday, 21st

Today is the celebration of the 100th day of the siege. People are having all sorts of pleasure in honour of the occasion, and one can almost fancy it is their desire to celebrate a 200th day.

Teacher Samson is very ill at the location. He has the rheumatic fever – the result of a bad cold his foot contracted while guarding on a rainy night.

This afternoon the Civil Commissioner held a meeting of the Barolongs in the stadt. Reuters and London *Times* war correspondents were also there. Things went on very smoothly until Wessels commenced to speak. He threw a different complexion on the otherwise excellent harmony which characterized the commencement of the proceedings. He misunderstood, misconstrued and misinterpreted everything said and an undesirable scene ensued.

I think he took serious exception to the suggestion by the Civil Commissioner that whoever desires to leave the place for the time being should be permitted to do so, as our supply of food is too limited. They both kept on talking, and scarcely gave each other a chance, each expecting me to translate his hot beans first. Whoever can interpret for Wessels correctly ought to consider himself a professor. Fancy having to either make an English speech, or to turn every word of the following half-sensible, broken Setswana parts of sentences and phrases, offered after peculiar intervals, into English:

'E' – 'ke a utlwa' – 'ke utlwa sentle' – 'jaka a bua' – 'ke re, morena' – 'a re . . .'[54]

Every one of these sentences causes him to assume a more

serious attitude. He will wave to and fro and occasionally change position and chair, or stand up to demonstrate his injured feelings. It is an excellent thing that the C.C. is so patient or else things could happen that would cause great joy in the Boer laager when they become known there.

Monday, 22nd

The same hammering by the big gun. [It is the] lot of a beleaguered community and we are awfully tired of it.

Tuesday, 23rd[55]

Shelling same as yesterday; all the shops have been closed as far as concerns the sale of everything edible, and the food is going to be rationed[56] out to the whites the same as the blacks in the grain stores.[57] The foreign women, perhaps, carry their parts with a grumble, but the leaders are announcing an offer for them to buy and [they] will be told that they can purchase tomorrow.[58] They say they will send back their tickets and ask for one which is available to buy any day.

This morning two were before the Court of Summary Jurisdiction. They were attempting to purchase with tickets belonging to other people. They pleaded ignorance and were dismissed with a caution.

Wednesday, 24th

There is a proclamation by the Colonel R. S. S. Baden-Powell that no food stores of any kind would in the future be sold to the public;[59] and white people are now going to buy food in rations and be compelled to buy small quantities, the same as blacks. I have often heard the black folk say money is useless as you cannot eat it when you feel hungry, and now I have lived it and experienced it. The thing appears to be going from bad to worse. The big gun is still hammering away at us. It was particularly cruel today. One of its shells hit on the Market Square this morning. It bumped right up in the air and singled out old Moshweshwe's hut (one-and-a-half miles away); after its decline it entered the hut from the back, decapitating two women and wounding three brothers severely and one not dangerously. The old boy was not there.

Thursday, 25th

Today was somewhat quiet. The Boers appeared to be short of Mauser ammunition. Sniping was not nearly as brisk as it was a month or two ago. At 2 p.m. Mafikeng[60] sent me some lovely stew and a few eggs for my supper in the evening. It arrived just while we were preparing our dinner and the former added to it, just made up, what one might call a splendid meal; and it was the same thing with the supper in the evening. Raseleye[61] kept repeatedly saying that he wondered why we are so lucky with food to have it falling into my direction; as it was the second anniversary of my wedding we enjoyed it all the more.

Friday, 26th

Malno arrived this morning but has greatly disappointed me as he has recently been to Kimberley. Finding the river impassable, he handed his despatches to Mr Honey of Skaapdam,[62] but he brought me a letter from the Imperial Government with the sad news of Ntsala Sakaria's demise.[63] This is particularly [unfortunate] coming as it does during Ebie's serious indisposition, and I am left to mourn his loss quietly by myself. The letter does not state when he died.

Sunday, 28th

The usual thing. In the middle of the morning the tranquillity of the neighbourhood was severely marred by the tolling of the warning bell. There was such a rush from town as has never . . .[64]

EDITORIAL NOTE

For the townspeople of Mafeking events took a serious turn for the worse during the month of January. For the first time the diarist conveys a mood of frustration; his attention is drawn increasingly to the civilian situation, its pathos and its bitterness. The many diaries kept during the period show neither the determined spirit of October and November, nor the (sometimes forced) cheerfulness of December. They speak rather of boredom and of growing physical hardship.

Whether or not Plaatje is right about the inexperience of the officers who supervised the production and distribution of food, it is interesting to speculate on how the encouraging situation of October gave way suddenly to the need for a frantic organization of supplies in January. The food predicament was symptomatic: many essential commodities were now being requisitioned. But the shortage was not restricted only to necessities. Equally threatening, albeit from a different point of view, was the shortage of ammunition. Remarkable work was undertaken by the ordinance workshop in this respect. Anything that had potential use as an explosive was suitably modified, and two artillery pieces were built. One was made with the gatepost from Rowland's Farm as its primary component; this curious object turned out to be an eighteenth-century, sixteen-pound naval gun, and after a clean-up was mounted and christened 'Lord Nelson' in honour of its seafaring past. The other, the 'Wolf' was constructed under the inspiration and direction of the artillery commander, Major Panzera. Like the gatepost gun, it turned out to have a longer range than expected. Together they were used to expand the perimeter of the besieged area so as to gain greater access to the desperately needed pasturage across the line of investment.

Slowly but inexorably the internal pressures on the garrison mounted. As they did, the Boer commander saw to it that bombardment from outside was intensified. From 1 January shelling had been greatly increased. It was well timed to induce a waning of morale. Yet things were still a long way from their lowest ebb. Sports and entertainments continued to provide the community with an opportunity to present a brave face. Ever faithful to the cause of morale-building, the tone of the *Mafeking Mail* remained cheerful. On the sixth it announced the relief of Ladysmith. That the report was false did not lessen its effect on the populace – at least, not until its unreliability was proved. But, beside its more encouraging information and announcements of pleasant events to come, reminders of the real situation stood out in grim relief. On the ninth the hoteliers published a notice to the effect that whisky prices were to rise to 1s 6d per glass (with other liquor increasing proportion-ately). Perhaps with a measure of irony, a 'Grand Agricultural and Produce Show' was announced for Sunday the twenty-first. The *Ther-mometer of Hope*, which marked the progress of relief troops on their way towards Mafeking, was rising. It was soon to lift the people to a pinnacle of hope – and then to drop them again into despair.

CHAPTER 4

February 1900

Tuesday, 6th

Got up this morning and found very lovely weather. 'Sanna' started at 9.00 and sent three shells into the town. I got there at 9.00 and met Sgt. Stuart who told me that the second shell burst in the Civil Commissioner's stable and smashed the stable, Whiskey[1] and all – poor fellow. When I got there I only saw his blood and nothing more of him, and a good thing too. A lot of Basutus[2] congregated on the spot, and hardly gave him time to die – so much in a hurry were they of getting his meat. They undoubtedly deprived the stadt of the best horse, and put me in a fix, as I doubt if poor Whiskey was a mere stroke of luck not likely to present itself again. I went to Phitshani,[3] 48 miles from here, with David one evening. He was sent there to get a horse and I merely accompanied him for pleasure. We had intended to be back at 8 o'clock the next morning, in time for court, as I went without leave. We were confident that David would easily perform the feat, or that I might accomplish it if he gave me the fresh horse we found at Phitshane. Poor Whiskey, however, landed me in Mafeking at 8 minutes past 8.00 and David with his two horses was not able to reach Mafeking before 11.30 – more than three hours later. I had been obliged to leave him at Libono, nearly 30 miles away; but this was nothing compared with the time we went to settle a land dispute between the boo Ratlou, when the Inspector of Native Reserves kept changing horses for five days – during which his horse was having a rest at Kraaipan.[4] It was, however, not able to carry him further than Maritzani on our return, and he had to give up riding and come home from that station by rail, as he could not keep up with me. He reached here at 4 p.m. per rail and I, on Whiskey, an hour after. It remains to be seen if I will be able to replace him.[5]

Mr Bell was saying, 'Poor creature, I was so sorry for him. He had not even murmured or done anything of the kind.'

Whiskey's fate was not our only grief today. The party of ten who went out to loot cattle returned this morning. Their expedition was a lamentable fiasco: it was most successful, though daring, right up to the last stage of its realization, but then the whole cart full of apples capsized.

They found that the cattle had been moved so deep into the Transvaal[6] that it would be impossible to reach Mafeking on the same night, if you left late in the evening, so they finally determined to tackle them shortly after sunset, and they did so last night. After the herds finished to milk, they went up to the kraal[7] and demanded its unconditional surrender. They shouted: 'Coang! Coang! ke tsa Morolong. Janong ga ithloli ele tsa Maburu!'[8] So saying, they pulled up some poles at the back of the kraal and started driving some cattle out. About 300 head were outside, when someone shouted that more than sufficient cattle were out already, and they should come away. Three of the party followed the cattle and the seven went for the Boers at the homestead, who had, by this time, been pouring a hail of Mauser bullets on the kraal. Our fellows soon silenced the Boers, but remained a little longer in order that the Boers should not know, too soon, which way the cattle went. I have forgotten to mention that the first shot here was fired at a young Dutchman, who was busy giving orders about the milking, and he fell on the spot. When they left, they saw another man lying dead near the kraal. They surely must have wounded some of them, for the fire of our little band silenced all their Mausers. There were also more than 20 head of cattle lying about which were wounded by the Boers!

So that it is not I only who is sorry today, but also a good many in Boer circles; besides, I will get compensation for poor Whiskey, although I preferred his 'isiqu'[9] to money, but who'll pay a Boer for 20 cattle? Oom Paul's bill is already large enough, and he is not likely to pay compensation to anybody, even if the loser prefers money to 20 head of cattle.

Returning to our subject, we will now devote our attention to the three fellows who left with the 300 head of cattle. They drove their cattle, thinking that the seven men would eventually overtake them. They drove the cattle till about 3.30 a.m., when they were very close to Mafeking – within two miles of our furthermost trench – and the Boers then stopped the cattle in front. They opened fire on the Boers and fought a desperate battle with good cheer, thinking that their comrades were somewhere behind, and would hurry up and reinforce them if they heard the shots. But this was not the case, and the Boers got the best of the game, as usual.[10] Our plucky three fellows had to come home disappointed.

Returning to the seven fellows, they walked on the track of the cattle, until one of them complained of sore feet. To leave him behind would have been too inhumane, and whilst they still went along, a piece of wood struck him in the foot, and they extracted it only with much difficulty. This delayed them, so that they weren't able to get on the track of their loot until it slipped out of the hands of the three men, back into the grasp of the enemy. They are confident that the pain and piece of wood in their comrade's foot were caused by Native 'peljase'[11] by which the owner of the farm (A. Lemmert, F.C.[12]) is protected. He and his family wear Native charms, and so do many of the Z.A.R. commandants and field-cornets. A Native M.D.[13] once got into trouble with his associates through having taught one of them how to use 'dolosse'.[14]

In the evening a chappie of the stadt was struck by a piece of shell on the head and is not expected to live. A little boy was out herding cattle and some Boer shot him on his forehead and the bullet came out at the back of his head. If he was struck by a Martini, then he would have been dead already. But a Mauser bullet being so small, he is still breathing.

We[15] have very great difficulty in feeding the Natives. There are about 7 000[16] of them in the stadt only, besides those at the location and the servants employed in the town. The grain supply is fast running short and it has been found necessary to stop giving oats to the horses and grind it for human food. Its first issue was this morning. There was a general murmur abroad which we hope by energetic surveyance soon to overcome, and to satisfy the discontented masses.

Wednesday, 7th

Up early.One gun is going strong in the west. The Boers have a little Maxim out there and this morning they poured a hailstorm of Mauser and Maxim ammunition at Fort Ayr.[17] If they had not been with us for nearly four months we would have imagined they are effecting an entry, but we have had hundreds of similar fusillades before and this cannot result in anything else but the same as before.

Moathloli[18] kindly lent me his Kolbooi[19] temporarily until I get another charge, but I am already tired of him. He is a good horse and 'takes the bun' as a trippelaar, but is slow – most piteously slow – and required considerable shoving along, which makes one very impatient and causes him to lose temper occasionally; particularly as he likes to stop every time he meets somebody.

The Boers have not done any damage today although there have been some marvellously narrow escapades.[20] Kolbooi feeds at the leg of the stable outside, and when a shell burst exactly ten yards past the stable it made me think that they are now going to kill every horse I keep. Capt. Fisher of the Town Guard came in shortly afterwards, frightened beyond measure. He was a few feet from the place where it burst.

Thursday, 8th

There was a little rain about 4.00 this morning and the weather is very enjoyable this morning.

Runners came in from the north. They bring good news as far as concerns Plumer's forces up north;[21] but nothing fresh from east and south.

'Au Sanna' went off during the middle of the morning but was quiet all day. I hear they were working at her all day. From today no Natives are allowed in town without a pass.[22] There are three classes of Natives, viz. permanent employees in town; permanent employees outside town; and stadt folk. The former (class one) are registered in the same manner as in Kimberley (the contract ticket) and walk about with a red ticket. I don't quite understand the procedure in class two. Class three receive a yellow ticket from Lekoko and hand it back every time they return from town.

I have started keeping an official diary from today, all of the doings in connection with Native affairs.[23] This is somewhat bothersome as besides this one I am typing Mr Bell's, Dr Hayes' and Capt. Greener's simultaneously. I cannot refuse the new gratis job as I am using the office typewriter and share the pay with no one; particularly as I heard the chief tell the Mayor that every member of this staff from his chief clerk down to the interpreter and every one of them [are] not only disinclined to do any work during the siege, but generally lodge a solemn protest and wish each to know the reason why he in particular, and not someone else, has to do that work.

The[24] people are now receiving oatmeal for food instead of grain which, it is feared, will run short if sure steps are not taken to save it. The oats were intended for horses, but as the horses could eat grass when things grow serious, it is being thought of as human food. There is a general grumble all round here also.

The pang has been felt all round, just at this time when folks had appetites. I have developed a marvellously strong appetite. I long for food every evening at 10.00 p.m. and after taking my supper at 7.00 I nearly die during the night if I do not take a cup of cocoa and a few biscuits before going to bed. Things are getting serious and I consider myself lucky for having thought out the thing at the beginning and stuffed my pants with matches and such things as were likely to be called in when things grow serious. I trust I will not number among those who will eat horses if we are not relieved by the end of March.[25]

Ganankoto[26] was for a little time the Civil Commissioner's great favourite. As he was often called: Hanangkutu; Mr One-Leg; Have-no-Nkutu; Habanab's or Have-no-Legs (from heav'n-o'-legs).

Friday, 9th

Very quiet day, although the smaller fry appeared to be part-icularly sharp – i.e. 'Grulle Annie'[27] and Mausers. We had only three shells from 'Au Sanna' today.

Runners came in from the south (Kimberley). Just strike out the item about Plumer in yesterday's northern despatches, and you have the news. They told me about Mr Gabriel[28] and family. They were with him as late as last week and his kids had been ill. Bob Moses was in Kimberley with them last month but he is ill. Elizabeth and Sainty [29] at 'Free State'. It is but a pity they[30] have never attempted to see any one of my relatives in Kimberley after deciding to come to Mafeking.

Although I am always doing my best to satisfy myself without Whiskey, Kolbooi always gives me cause to regret his fate. For instance this evening I was coming from town. There was a small curve behind the hedge at the railway camp round which I wanted to turn him. He was tripelling very fast and as he is loath to turn quickly he ran plump into the wire fence. I 'tlolela'[31] on one side and stood watching him tangling himself with the wire, until I did not for a moment think he would come out with a sound leg. If he was sensible he would take a lesson from today and stop always looking in the air as though he is smoking a cigar. Disobedience was the cause of this mishap.

Mathakgong[32] went out with four others.

Saturday, 10th

Things are looking mighty blue. Colonel Baden-Powell states

he has received a message from Lord Roberts that we will not be relieved for another three months yet and that he has not got any food for any but Barolongs, the white people and fixed residents of the place. He is therefore going to shut up the town grain store, which was only used for refugees, who came here from Johannesburg before the war, imagining that the war was going to be a matter of days.

He is going to give them only ten days grace after which he is going to close all stores, and also shut the door against their employment at the defence works, where gangs of hundreds of them are employed every day and night. These people include Bangwaketse, Bakwena, Zulus, Zambesians, Shangaan, and others too numerous to mention. The Civil Commissioner has suggested that letters be written to Bathoen[33] and he be asked to communicate with Gnl. Snyman requesting him to let his people come out of Mafeking, as he is on friendly terms with the Boers. By this means of course many people, including Barolongs, who will only be too pleased to go to Kanya can leave this beleaguered place. A letter will also be sent to Colonel Plumer asking him to be in touch with Bathoen at Kanya and arrange with him to give the people some reward for clearing out of here. It was proposed that Major Goold-Adams should write to Bathoen and so should Wessels: the latter, however, refused to have anything to do with the thing.

There appears to be something very deadly about second shells. The second shell this morning went into Mr Dall's house. It found him standing near the kitchen and fractured the lower half of his body; only his upper half was alright. This is very sad. It was only yesterday that I was talking with Mr Dall[34] for the first time since the siege and he said he was wondering where I had been all the four months.

In the evening some of our people (12) from our advance trench, two miles south of the stadt, went out to annoy the Boers. They passed out unobserved and were only fired on on their return. They returned the fire and the Boers fled and were quite silent for the rest of the night.

Sunday, 11th

Today was just as usual. A man came from Gopane's[35] and reports Snyman had gone up country to fight Plumer as his Dutch opponents were very 'slecht'[36] and generally good for nothing. This afternoon we sent out four runners, two in each direction (north and south).

At 11.00, before we turned in, there was a perfect fusillade. It was a Mauser volley and as they were quickly followed by Martinis we became confident that it was Mathakgong coming in. As they continued, the Mausers remained silent and our belief was firm. Mr Raseleji ran across and found the whole plain alive with armed men making for the scene of operations. And our belief was only too true. He was coming in with 12 head, and on approaching, found that the Boers were themselves on two sides, and had presumably sworn that it was the 'verdomde kaffers' fag end, for directly the cattle [were] exactly between, they opened fire with heavy volleys from right and left. Four men returned the fire on the right, and Mathakgong that on the left. What do you think the lot of Boers did? They ran away.

Their volleys wounded two oxen – one fell on the spot and the second fell just inside our advance trench. First-class beef for our snipers and Mathakgong brought home ten. These few were all they could find about Maritzani, all of the Boer cattle having been moved deep into the Transvaal. They were probably a span of oxen which strayed from their wagon. May God have mercy on their Native herd!

Monday, 12th

This is the hottest day we have had for a long time. Shelling was very mild during last week and all was quiet till after nine this morning. They probably had a raad[37] about the cattle that came in, as I am sure their number was put down at 50 or 70 and the number of the escort ditto – for surely if they told Snyman that the cattle were driven by only five men they would receive a thrashing and be branded as cowards. To allow only five Kaffirs to pass their lines with cattle! The big gun opened after 9.00 and did its level best to hit numbers of cattle grazing south of the Molopo – and failing to hit them, it went for the town. Presumably with the object of giving us cayenne pepper and mustard to add to the ox meat we were having, but without result. The only casualty for the day was one with far-reaching effect. While Mr (now Captn.) Girdwood, in charge of the supplies, etc., was coming from his home [he] received a bullet in the stomach and is not expected to live longer than a day. Mr E. K. Grayson, B.A.,[38] has been appointed in his place.

There was a heavy fire all round about the Boers, which gave us the opinion that our runners will not get through, and so it proved, for they all came back this morning. The brickfields . . .[39]

Tuesday, 13th

Captn. Girdwood died today. He was a very old Mafekingite, having been a customs officer even for the Imperial Government before the annexation.[40] He was appointed to take charge of the food only a month ago, and he did his best to bring about a desirable satisfaction amongst the Barolong. To attain that object, he sent the storeman away, and introduced a very good-natured fellow who gets along with Barolongs in a most excellent manner. They are most sorry at his death.

The Boers have brought another kind of shell to bear on us. They have incensed[41] the 9-pounder shells and they are very incendiary.[42] Yesterday we saw a flame in the course of one of the shells [in the air] to where it exploded. The flame went out before it reached the ground. These shells struck at Mrs Stenson's, and the explosion caused fire. That must be the reason why they have started shelling the stadt – apparently to test its effect on the grass-thatched huts. They continued the shelling till 10 p.m. and knocked off, presumably disgusted, for no damage was done, and they have become mild again. They are, I think, perfectly convinced that there is nothing in them, for if they were of any use, and if the flames were effective, they certainly ought to have seen the grass huts blaze away in the dark night. However, after one of those shells exploded, Manomphe's son-in-law, Thlaping, walked up, and while picking up a fragment, noticed that there was something like a cut diamond[43] in the debris. He picked up this beauty of a thing. His nerve, however, told him that there was danger in it but, in order to do justice to his pluck, he took his left hand full of sand and put this thing on it. The sand caught fire and burnt his hand. He chucked away this thing and rubbed his burning left hand with his right. The former ignited the latter, and he was soon tortured with pain. His only relief is to keep his hands in cold water – this does not help much unless fresh water is put in every three minutes, for the water becomes very hot after it.

Wednesday, 14th

Ebie's birthday – I have not done anything for it, as I have since night before last got a most excruciating pain in the foot. I never thought rheumatism had such a sharp pain. I have been writing this all through it.

The Colonel sent a hot message to Lekoko saying that he and his people did very wrong in slaughtering the cattle[44] without giving the commissariat a chance of buying any of them. His answer was no 'cooler'. 'We have been giving you a fourth of all the loot, and you said you did not care for it.'[45]

Thursday, 15th

Today was like the day on which the big gun arrived. Consternation was written in bold and expressive type in the face of everybody in the stadt. The gun had been moved from its position round to the south-west of the stadt, about 5 miles away, and therefore 6½ miles from town. The Limestone fort, women's laager, and the stadt are therefore going to be its restless victims.

It tested its range at about 10.30 and fell short of the Limestone fort. No. 2 burst unpleasantly aside of the fort, and 3 made head for the stadt; 4 missed Mamolateli; 5 and 6 plumped into the women's laager and 7 went for the old Wessels (Senobe's) house. It smashed the passage shelter, killing two Bangwaketse women, who happened to be about, and wounding one. All the others fell promiscuously about the stadt. These shells came in rapid succession, and at noon there was two hours' respite. At 2 p.m. they sent over two more, which failed to reach town. At 5 p.m. they sent their last, which fell in the stadt, and fortunately did not burst.

Thus was the début of 'Au Sanna's' undesirable entertainment. They loaded after five, but although the bells kept us expectant she was quiet for the evening. I am inclined to the belief that the spot they have chosen lastly is uncomfortable for them. Three miles was a bad range for them from which to try to hit the town, but 6½ miles is still worse. We surely cannot understand why the Boers should go and place the gun so far away – and that on the further side of the Transvaal border. The general idea is that nothing is daunting them and they see that it stands in absolutely no danger whatever of being molested, and completely drives away all expectations of relief for us.[46] But there is something else. There was a flag of truce coming from Snyman's laager. One Cape Policeman went to meet it. It was a message from Snyman and the bearer of it told our policeman that there had been a serious battle in Natal. On our man asking who took the day the bearer said he did not know: this message said the writer has instructed the burghers that if in future the inhabitants should expose themselves on Sundays they should fire on them. One can almost think that he is going to Kimberley with the big gun on Sunday and does not want us to see a considerable portion of his laager trekking.

Friday, 16th

The stadt has [for] once changed from its usual appearance and assumed a sullen aspect. We have not experienced it yet, but if the long look for the greatest day is unequalled, today was undoubtedly a second study of judgement day. People were almost disinclined to talk to one another, and there was dead silence in the green shrubbery which almost gave one the impression that on other days they were talkative. I spent my day in old Watermann's garden, without food of any sort: it was only [when] she, grand lady, brought me several sweet cones [that I could] break my fast. I felt very stimulated after being invigorated by them and tired of novel reading and shorthand exercises. I still retained a fresh enough memory to picture to myself the figure of a very young mother and a fat little piccaninny disturbing her peace (assisted by the absence of someone) somewhere about the Eastern Province.[47]

Shelling was going on very lively, and fully justified the people's looks in the morning. The big gun only put in a few, but the show was generally kept up by the incendiary 9-pounders which put in about 30 during the day. It fired from Jackal Tree where it was on the morning that it killed poor Mamokoloi. It, however, went for our defence works like it ought to do. It went almost invariably for the forts of McKenzie's Black and the Barolong Watches – within two miles of the stadt. The former is on the railway line and the latter one mile west of it.

Only the big gun went promiscuously for the stadt, and one woman at my friend Moathloli's house was only saved [from being decapitated] by a hair's breadth. The shell smashed the wall of the hut, burst inside it then found means of exit through another wall behind which the woman was sitting. One piece burst right opposite her head, but unlike the others it rebounded and fell inside. When the woman bowed her head a lot of earth fell from it and there was a hole in the wall.

The 'bad-night' shot was fired at 8.45. Emang[48] had brought us tea early in the evening. At 8.00 I went home with her. I found

Mafikeng sitting near the north-eastern corner of her house against the rising moon. We had not yet chatted to our heart's content when there was heavy rifle firing to the west. We had hardly passed remarks over it when 'tingalingalingaling' chimed the tocsins[49] and we dodged like a couple of meercats. There was a heavy suspense when we were waiting for the blow – I think 20 seconds – when bang went a terrible smash. Then the usual row, terminating in a loud explosion that echoed through all the neighbourhood. Nothing would induce Mafie to remain to the open air and I believe she wanted to be dismissed for directly I suggested she should take to the shelter she leapt and bounded towards it with no less alacrity than Malibali[50] or Emang could have mastered. I went round to see what [it] was like inside. The whole family was arraigned in it. There was old Masiako,[51] the two girls and two old dames, and goodness knows too what more. This refuge was luminated with a candle that the old dame had sent Mamoathloli[52] for just one hour previously. I strolled back to our quarters and jotted down these notes, while the evening was kept up by the usual rifle chatter which is forever the case in bright moonlight.

Saturday, 17th[53]

Our troops kept up fire all night. The Maxim was going nobly all the time. By midnight it had become one of the grandest nights, watching our rifle flashes like a lot of fireworks to the south. Our volleys going for the Boers all night were worth listening to. We were pressing away all night: the bright moonlit night being kept alive by the bombs of the 7-pounders and Nordenfeld, the cracks of rifles, and the tat-tat-tat of the firing. The Boers had worried the souls out of us during the day;[54] and it is particularly consoling to see that they did it at the expense of their rest the next night. Not a single Dutch weapon was to be heard above the occasional Mauser or rifle.

We had a very quiet day. One often wondered if they exhausted themselves yesterday. 'Au Sanna' sent in a few shells to the women's laager.

Sunday, 18th[55]

The usual thing. Runners came in from up north-east and south. They brought no news. It is difficult to describe one's feeling hearing that even now after four months Kimberley has not yet been relieved. The Imperial Government may be as good as we are told it is, but one thing certain is that it does not care a hang over the lives of its distant subjects. It is distressing to hear that troops are still having a holiday at Modder River,[56] even now after we had been besieged over four months. In Kimberley, which is only a stone's-throw from Cape Town, they were still eating horseflesh with 10 000 troops at Modder River, and we may safely conclude that we, as far away as Mafeking, will have no more horseflesh to eat by the time they reach here.

The cattle and green mielie stocks have also been called in. No one is allowed to pick any green mielies for his or her village. They are going to be kept till they are ripe and then rationed out to people.

I am wondering if the heavens, like the Imperial Government, have also shut their ears to our prayers. Surely: 'Eare bo bisa go bitsa motho, go bitse molimo.'[57] But was this so in our case?

I have a very strong appetite just now when food is very scarce. If I do not take a cup of cocoa at 10 p.m. (after suppering in the evening at 7) you may depend upon it I will never be able to sleep. This is an undesirable bad habit, and I almost feel inclined to consult the medico about it.[58]

Monday, 19th

As quiet as last Saturday. 'Sanna' only sent in two shells (7 a.m.) which fell short of the town. The day was uneventful.

Tuesday, 20th

When the pass law was introduced for the time being I expected we would have about 20 convictions every week. We have up to date not had any infringers before the court. In fact when one is found minus the pass the policemen simply tell him to clear out of town.

'Au Sanna' sent in three miserable shots this morning. I believe there is something wrong with her. Only one of them burst and some people mistook the explosion for a Krupp 9-pounder's. One of them went into Moathloli's again but did no damage.

One medico of Mafeking (Dr Smythe) was, at the commencement of the row, appointed to doctor over the inmates of the women's laager. He had the funks and declined the appointment, fearing to leave his bomb-proof any day except Sundays. He has since been living at his house, which was also struck by a 94-pounder last week. I wonder where he intends going.

Wednesday, 21st[59]

A calm and unusually lovely day! Eventually I got up early and went to town, returning at 12, and spent the day in the gardens. Joshua[60] caught a thief in these gardens. He was a heathen, and in a farmer's employ. They nearly beat him to death. I returned to town again at 4.00, and found Weil's crowded with Fingoes and Zambezians, with no consciousness of the fact that the town store had closed its doors last night,[61] and that they could get no more food. They are only too anxious to avail themselves of the opportunity of going over to Kanya, as offered by the authorities. They were worrying me, and waiting for me to give them passes, when one of them fell in the courtyard of starvation – the poor fellow was taken to the hospital, where he died afterwards.

Thursday, 22nd

One of the greatest troubles I have endured during the siege is that I have been put on rations. Thus food becomes one of the greatest desires of a man's dreams, on it he would spend all his money if he could.[62]

Today I am simply going to fetch the newspaper and receive my week's suppply without any fuss. It consists of 7×1 lb tins of preserved meat, 1 lb of sugar, half-a-pound of tea, ½ lb of coffee, some salt, pepper, rice, meal, etc. The greatest care is exercised that one should get as little as possible of everything.

It was urgently suggested that surpluses be held for the starving people to eat, but it was this day discovered that there was sufficient oatmeal to keep them going and undesirable foodstuff has not yet been introduced. We hope it will never be. In town the thing is being done already.

The big gun has been shifted from its position west of the stadt and is now in its southerly place, as near as the Malmani[63] road. It has, however, not fired a single shot today. This is only the third holiday that 'Au Sanna' has given us since her arrival.

I have not mentioned that Sgt. Major Looney, of the garrison, was taken in on the 7th instant. He was tried[64] last Saturday by court martial, which I witnessed for the first time. Major Godley was presiding, and all the others present were dressed in their best uniforms. The court was crowded, and I left it still in progress. Sentence was deferred until today. Looney was arraigned on the Market Square and sentence was promulgated by Major Godley.[65] According to the newspaper on Tuesday, we were allowed to be present at the promulgation. He was sentenced to

be reduced from the ranks of His Majesty's Service and to serve
five years' penal servitude. The securities[66] turned round and
dismissed him, and he was handed over to the civil powers. I felt
so sorry for him – such a pretty young fellow. I understand that
he has a wife and child. His face is exactly like Mamasinoke's.[67]
He is a white Ralisa. Lovely rains fell in the night.

Friday, 23rd

The big gun discharged seven shots during the morning. She
was trying to hit a number of cattle that were grazing to the north
of the town, but did not hit any.

About 100 Boers were seen to go north during the day. The
whole of the day was very quiet. A fair, still and cloudy evening.
No 'bad-night shot' this evening.

Saturday, 24th

It was raining all night through. The morning in consequence
is very lovely. It has been abnormally quiet all these days. But
today was extraordinary. We could see early this morning that
the weather would keep the Boers quiet and that was really the
case. Fine soaking rains were the order of the day. Mausering
and shelling were absent and the warning bell for the firing of
the big gun was conspicuous in its silence. It was quite a holiday
and many of us during our movements quite forgot the big gun's
presence.

Sunday, 25th

The veldt looks quite green and lovely after yesterday's rains. I
have not mentioned that during the week Snyman wrote to say
that he was notifying us for the last time with regard to the
Sunday, as he sees that far from worshipping God we use it as a
day of building forts, chopping wood and sending out 'maids'
and children with passes signed by 'den heer Belle',[68] who was
formerly or still is Magistrate of Mafeking and who at one time
was refused by Kapitein Wessels, well knowing that Baden-
Powell was the head official – and other such rubbish.[69] (I
wonder if he means that Mr Bell should not sign passes, but
should leave that duty to the O.C.) Therefore anyone showing
himself on this day, or cattle going beyond their week-day's
grazing lines, and officers reconnoitring too far will be fired on
by his burghers.

In the morning there were several shots, and there was some

Mausering to show us that Snyman was true to his word. But towards the middle of the morning all was just as calm as usual.

Runners came in from the north. They brought bad news. We are anxiously awaiting the relief of Ladysmith and Kimberley.[70] As the last *Mail* stated General Roberts was going to the front,[71] we are expecting an account and result of his trip with big eyes. Wires came from Bulawayo to say that the telegraph between Salisbury and Beira was out of order and that is the reason why there is no news worth recording. Two Dutchmen escaped from here and went to the Boers during the day. They think their side is going to be victorious but as the relief of the above-mentioned towns is expected shortly, they have just left in good time to discover their folly. A Native from the Boers states that Snyman had been away up north when the big gun was turned around to the west, and he ordered its return.

Monday, 26th

A spy returned from Lothlakane this morning. He brought good news. Kimberley has been relieved during the second week in February and the line is being constructed north of Kimberley. This news, it appears, was brought to Rietfontein by a young fellow who left this place with Cronje's commandos, and he states that Cronje was shot through the shoulders when the relief of Kimberley was effected. Poor fellow. We will get Transvaal for the Major-Genl. Lord Methuen's wounds. I wonder what the Boers are going to get for his shoulders.[72]

Tuesday, 27th

On horseback all day, gathering people together and arranging for their exodus tonight.[73]

A letter was sent to Genl. Snyman telling him to (1) remove all of the armed Natives away from Mafeking; (2) restore Saane[74] back to his people at Molimola, failing which he should consider the old agreement – that Natives should take no part in the fight – at an end: Bathoen, Pula, Sechele, Ikaneng, Lenchwe, Kgama (all of the Protectorate Chiefs) would be permitted to enter the Transvaal and loot farms at random. This would be a grand affaire for even the Bahurutshe[75] would not sit still. This would be the Dutch people's final crush – at least round here. They had enough to do with Colonels Plumer and Baden-Powell, when they each had about 1 000 men. Just now they must be considered to be in a dilemma as to how they should oppose these two heads[76]

– and what more if all these chiefs who are all more or less dreaded by Marico Boers should reinforce them? 'Humanity will shudder', to use Jabavu's [77] phrase.

At 4 p.m. there were about 400 men and women gathered near the railway bridge and more were arriving by scores.

At 6 p.m. there were about 900 of them. A waggon-load of mule flesh arrived and each received a piece. At 7.00 it was discovered, after a second load had arrived, that there was not yet sufficient meat for the crowd.

I saw horseflesh for the first time being treated as human foodstuff. It looked like meat with nothing unusual about it, but when they went to the slaughter-pole for the third time and found that there was no more meat left and brought the heads and feet, I was moved to see their long ears and bold heads, and those were the things the people are to feed on. The recipients, however, were all very pleased to get these heads and they ate them nearly raw. After 7 they began to move in the direction of the B.S.A. camp. The Civil Commissioner, who arrived on the scene half-an-hour earlier, looked like their Moses, and Private (now Sergeant) Abrams, C.P.,[78] their Aaron. The latter is in charge of the stadt guard. He had been with the Barolongs since the commencement of the wars and the bravery which character- ized him has distinguished him before his officers and gained for him a profound respect before all Barolongs. When one of them feels hungry and remembers that his hunger is a part of the siege, he generally gets disgusted at the English way of going to work, which involves the prolongation of the trouble, and exclaims that there are only two good and brave Englishmen in this world – and they are Balofete (Lt.-Colonel Walford) and Aberamo.

When this matter was got up it was directed that Sgt. Abrams and 12 of his men should accompany these people only as guides to show them the way and urge them on. Two detachments of the Protectorate Regiment were to keep their right and left flanks and do all the firing in case any Boer fires at them. We passed the B.S.A. camp, went on to Fort Cardigan and further on past Fort Miller[79] – places which I and Mr Bell have never been, not even on a Sunday, since the commencement of the siege – and still there was no sign of the volunteers. We went along until we found only the O.C. and two or three other officers – but no volunteers.

It is doubtful if there ever was an exodus so momentous as the one on the day on which Israel came out of Egypt: the house of

Jacob from people of a strange language; when Judah was his sanctuary and Israel his dominion. But if brother Moses was in Mafeking this evening he would himself admit that these people's exodus gave more work or thought, considering that they are flying from a common enemy, starvation, and they do not expect to travel three miles before being fired on by another enemy – the Boers. The Israelites, for instance, when they left Pharaoston[80] (Kharthoum, Cairo or wherever it was) were driven out by the enemy with the approval of everyone in authority. But this unfortunate 900 we want to get rid of, and that is why we are sending them away to Canaan where we have 'milk and honey', green makatane,[81] etc., which are really milk and honey compared with the mule-flesh in store for them; but we have not consulted the Boers who are at present in authority and [who] will surely have things quite their own way. This disadvantage the Moses–Aaron crew did not have. (Their provisions were lamb, veal, and no horseflesh.)[82]

When a start was made from the river, there arose cries of 'Mma, Mma', children shouting after their mothers, and women after their children in the dark: but after passing the B.S.A. camp, besides the heavy treads of twice 900 feet, there reigned a dead silence.

After our return we waited and heard a few Mauser volleys in the direction in which they went. I did not wait till I turned in, for at about 11.30 Matshenko knocked at the door (every inmate of the Shankaan[83] had joined the exodus) and told me that all that elaborate arrangement had burlesqued. The volunteers failed to turn up and 12 men being unable to very well fight and drive 900 people at the same time, the Boers scattered the whole crowd in every direction. This was a serious blow to me particularly, taking into consideration that I have been on horseback from early till late during the last two days – and all that for 'niks'.[84] I turned in at 12.00, took a short nap, then heard Taelo[85] waking men with the statement that the Barolongs are now going to take them out and I should accompany them – a perfect nuisance.

It was decided to bring them back and keep them in the hollow at Maphachwe[86] until the next evening when they will be taken out by Natives. They were guarded all night by armed men and were not permitted to return to the stadt.

This is a matter of such a sweeping importance as puts all other questions in the dark.

Wednesday, 28th[87]

It has at last been resolved that Barolongs should attack down at the trenches by night. We spent much of the day with them there. Six men reported themselves as having come from the Boers. They left home on Monday night. They were fired at by the Boers who eventually got them, and told them to return to Mafeking and leave in broad daylight if they wish to save their lives. They appear quite confident of getting back there if they were allowed to have it their way and it was resolved to [let them] do so in the morning. Mr Bell's horse is still gone.[88]

EDITORIAL NOTE

The month of February was not distinguished by great events or outstanding deeds. It is perhaps true that from the British point of view the month ended with a slight military credit-balance: Fort Cronje, which lay a mile to the south of the stadt and had formerly been an important Boer sniping-post, was captured. Apart from partially solving the persistent problem of inadequate grazing-land, this also reduced the effectiveness of Boer positions on the southern front. It brought the meagre British artillery to within range of Jackal Tree and other nearby fortifications. But the problems of physical hardship and boredom were growing more acute. A resolute front continued to be shown to a world which watched but could not see.

The townspeople only now began to experience what the Barolong had known the month before. Horseflesh began to feature regularly on the family menu. In the stadt malnutrition diseases (and, on occasion, fatalities) were spreading amongst the people, as is evidenced by the decision to evacuate refugees to Kanye.

The news of the relief of Kimberley at the end of the month could not have come at a better time for beleaguered Mafeking. It was followed by a significant leap in the *Thermometer of Hope* as relief became a more immediate possibility.

The various siege-journals stress the fact that community organization continued to improve, that the defensive system was becoming more and more difficult to breach and that both the civilian and the military populations were determined to retain a high level of morale. One suspects, however, that these were written with a knowledge that history was in the making. Patriotic 'heroism', expressed in optimistic statements, obscures the essential point which may be adduced from Plaatje's February entries: that, behind the resolute front, hunger and fear were becoming potent enemies. General Snyman's policy was at last having noticeable effect.

CHAPTER 5

March 1900

Thursday, 1st

A fine cloudy morning. Just remembered that I am now commencing my seventh year in the service.[1] This has been the busiest week I have had since the siege [began]. Thirty of the refugees were sent out this morning. They went right up to Game Tree where the Boers received them, it appeared, quite cheerfully.

Friday, 2nd

We are still very busy with the food matter. It is proposed to erect a place in the stadt where soup will be cooked for the benefit of the poor. It is soup made of oatmeal and horseflesh and as there are a great many hungry people in the place they each receive a good feed gratis.

The big gun pumped in a lot of shells in the morning, but as it was raining during the day, shooting was consequently very mild.

I heard in the afternoon that 'Au Sanna' had been taken to the parapet.[2] They are probably moving her somewhere else. In the evening at about 8.00 our Nordenfeld started bombing and kept up his patter incessantly. One could simply conclude that someone saw them putting the big gun up somewhere in the vicinity. It was very grand to listen to master Nordenfeld's 'ptions-ptions-ptions'. We have not heard it for a long time.

Saturday, 3rd

Early this morning 'Au Sanna' opened fire on the brickfields. She is back at her old position opposite the Nordenfeld's, across the Makane valley and therefore miserably close to the brickfields. By 7 o'clock she had already put in 41 shells and then[3] 'shut up' after wounding Sgt.-Major Taylor and two others so severely that he is not expected to live. Taylor's case is pretty sad for he was one of the best men we had in the place.[4] He worked his way quietly to the brickfields until he took his position after killing a considerable number of Boers. It was only last week that he told me that if he knew that 'such conditions' were awaiting him in Mafeking, he would never have come up here.

One of 'Au Sanna's' gunners was shot today and he died on the spot. Two more were wounded at the brickfields and another of the Bechuanaland Rifles. These are all we ourselves saw and there are probably many more. The range of our big guns appears very effective. (The above-mentioned were killed by Maxims.) They have taken off the big gun again and we wonder where it has gone this time. This has been an unfortunate day for Boer, British, etc. The Sidzumos lost cattle very heavily – 14 all told. Eight killed and six wounded. One poor brute's nose was completely ripped off. It was a mess and I had often drunk her milk.

The commissioner's department bought the whole lot. Old Sidzumo[5] wanted to have cattle at the end of the war, but was told that that is an impossibility.

Sunday, 4th

This was another unfortunate day.[6] Sgt.-Major Bill (Colonial Contingent) was wounded on the arm and a Morolong scout attached to the C.P.[7] was shot through the neck. These things occurred at the brickfields. It being Sunday, they walked out of their trenches and exposed themselves, and that is how they were shot. The Boers must be getting some nasty knocks somewhere for they now don't care a hang about worshipping their God on Sundays. The rattling of Mausers today was just as brisk as on ordinary week-days. I went to town and also to Maphacoe[8] where I found a little boy who had been out eating 'moretlwa'[9] with two others. They were fired on by the Game Tree Boers who wounded him[10] through both thighs and one arm. He could not say what became of the other two.

Runners came in and confirmed the news about the relief of Kimberley and also that our friend Cronje is in a tight fix at Jacobsdal[11] and the troops expect to catch him. Some Boers up north have retired before Colonel Plumer at the Crocodile Pools.

Monday, 5th[12]

The big gun is said to be back. It is near McMullen's. There was some very brisk volleying in the direction of the brickfields, and we hear that the 'Kaapenaars'[13] have vacated their position there. Captains FitzClarence and Williams, with several men, rushed the place, and took it, minus any casualties.

Poor Taylor died during the day. Few people who have not been in Mafeking during the raid will understand how valuable his services have been to the garrison. He had been as plucky a soldier of His Majesty's during the siege as he has been the lowly servant of Christ in the English church in times of peace. He was part of the military force, and his funeral is to be attended by the Officer Commanding, and other officers of the garrison.

A man left here on Saturday last for Kanya. He was fallen upon by the Boers, who, on catching him, sent him back to Mafeking. The Natives had been disarmed, they told him, and were going back to their homes.[14] The Boers were also going to leave the place, and camp at the border. He saw them actually loading up, and the preparations clearly indicated that they were going to leave. This has still to be proved, although we could not altogether disbelieve him, as these Boers have surely not come here for life.

Tuesday, 6th

A beautiful morning. 'Au Sanna' was silent all the morning, and only opened fire effectively at 4.00 p.m. Many people were taken in when they saw the dummy gun,[15] and no 'Sanna'. Last week we made them waste a waggon-load of shells by pressing the dummy truck on the long-disused railway line, near Mr B. W.[16] I saw the chimney-pipe sticking out of it, so that it looked like the armoured train. Sometimes a 'Guy Fawkes' is constructed outside one of the trenches and made to jump about by means of strings fixed to him, as this would draw out showers of Mauser ammunition. We will do anything to remind the Boers of the dynamite trick of the 13th October, and we have done a lot of harm to the Boers with this sort of thing.

'Au Sanna' let off two shots during the day; punctually at 4.00 and 6.00 p.m. respectively.

Wednesday, 7th

A very quiet day. The bells rang twice, but 'Au Sanna' never fired.

Thursday, 8th

Very good news in the morning by runners from the north and messengers from Saane's.[17]

Boers   Recapture of Colesberg
bolted   Dordrecht taken at the point of bayonets.
before
Buller
Glorious slaughter of women slayers.[18]
Brilliant onslaught on women murderers.[19]

Cronje's term as 'general'[20] is at its final stage – 1 000 Boers killed around him and 7 000 taken prisoner with him.

Mathakgong and his band are coming tonight with a hundred beautiful cattle they espied near Maritzani.

Snyman disarmed the Rietfontein rebels[21] who now wonder where they'll go. Malan has retired in front of Colonel Plumer who is at Lobatsi[22] and Snyman leaves Mafeking with Malan tomorrow.

'Au Sanna' let off once, at 8 this morning.

Friday, 9th

'Au Sanna' never let off a shot today. It may be because they are short of ammunition or that, their gunner being shot, no one is able to control the gun.

Some women went out in the direction of Signal Hill[23] to gather green makatane, etc., from their fields. They saw a few young Boers who told them to glean in haste and return before their parents come as they will not permit them to take away any. Mathakgong has not turned up yet.

Saturday, 10th

'Sanna' fired two shots in the morning. Nothing eventful. The horse thieves sentenced.[24]

Sunday, 11th

Mathakgong came in this morning. Since they left here they spent the week very close to Madibe siding.[25] During the week they sent six men to a neighbouring farm to steal some goats. Four men came back with a sheep in the evening, the fifth turned up next morning, and the sixth failed to put in an appearance until they left their camp. On Friday they saw a mounted man coming past their camp, with a packet of dynamite in his hand. He left his horse, then walked towards the railway line. One man wanted to shoot him as he bent over the line, but the others refused as he was unarmed. How unlike the Boers, who would shoot any one of us without hesitating to find out if he was armed. After this they heard a loud explosion and the man did this a second and third time. He was blowing up the line. When he returned they recognized him as old 'Barwise' of the farm Rooidammetjies.[26] It was at once resolved that his cattle should be taken.

On Saturday evening they attacked his farm, drove the Boers, servants, dogs, etc., out of the homestead and then took the cattle. They wanted to get hold of the calves but when they opened the kraal (during the heat of the fire) the calves jumped out at the back and followed their running owners.

Three horses that were tied there also did the same and they only came away with the cattle – 27 fat animals. The journey was uneventful. They had intended to cross the Boer lines a little to the east of the old railway line but by mistake they came too high and were surprised to find themselves at the Jackal Tree Boer fort, where the Boers opened fire on them. Mathakgong shouted at the top of his voice:

'Likganela re li loele. Ba tshega bare re basimane ba likoalo ba ba senang go iphemela. Maburu a, ebile Manyesemane a ba lamalitse ka go ba neela fela yaka ba rata lieme re li loele.'[27]

On hearing this one of the Boers mounted a grey horse and swifted off towards their western fort, shouting for reinforcements. But the battle was already on then. They fought their way through and lost one man, killed – poor Maiku was a very plucky fellow. He left here in December at a time when we knew nothing of what goes on in Kimberley and he reached Kimberley, returned, and brought us news about the true state of affairs there. The Boers killed one ox. Our men killed two Boers that they saw, and heard one screaming some distance to the left. He screamed for a long time – till our men had left Jackal Tree far behind.

Things are getting very strained now. People cannot get any cattle without having to risk very much. Another party went out last night and Teacher Potiphar is going out tonight with 24 men. He has since the beginning performed brilliant services and has always taken a part in whatever act the Barolongs distinguished themselves with during the siege. We hope he will do as well in the veldt.[28]

Monday, 12th
Paul[29] took 50 men and attacked a Dutch fort about three miles to the south of the stadt last night. As they were leaving they sent

a man to Captn. Marsh[30] for ammunition but he came back saying Captn. Marsh was not there so they had to go and attack the place with about three to seven rounds of ammunition per man. Fortunately they went round and reached the further end of the trench unobserved until they opened fire on the sleeping Boers. There was a sudden scramble for the wall, but numbers of them were knocked down by bullets while in the act of climbing over the fence. The battle was very successful and just at the time they would have taken the fort they were obliged to leave it on account of their ammunition being all spent. They are certain of eight killed Boers besides the lot that were screaming and groaning in the fort.

'Au Sanna' went for us during the morning, probably endeavouring to shell their cattle out of us. The cannon has been very quiet all week and this sudden waking up is very undesirable as we have already got unused to it.

Two cattle-looting parties are still at large and we hope if they are as successful as Mathakgong we will frighten the Boers away from here as they will fancy that the whole of their country is simply swarming with armed Natives.

Women are now always going out to Moleloane[31] and coming home with a lot of melons and kaffircorn, so we are wondering why the Boers permit them to get out so far while they have not previously even been allowing them to go out to get some bushes for fuel behind the convent on Sundays. Some of the women get driven back but go round and try somewhere else and come back successful.

Tuesday, 13th

More news – all of it good. Ladysmith[32] has been relieved by General Sir R. Buller who, although he lost somewhat heavily, killed 2 000 Boers and took 3 000 prisoners.

Some of our cattle raiders came back. Their trip was interesting though accompanied by misfortunes, and they had a warm time of it yesterday. After leaving Mafeking, 'Luiku' and the northerner Colbourne Msikinya[33] could not agree with the majority of the party, and he turned towards Polfontein[34] with the royal following of six all told. Eighteen men went towards Madibe and the following were their adventures: during the middle of the morning they saw 11 Boers riding all along their spoor towards the koppie on which they were sheltered. They hid rightly behind some stones until the Boers came on the koppie. One of the Boers saw them. They exchanged fire and the Boers ran away leaving one man and a horse killed.

They knew the Boers would go for reinforcements, so they decided they should go to a hole in the open plain round Madibe siding. Entrenched in a hole they would, of course, have the Boers at their mercy as there is absolutely nothing behind which to take cover. They refreshed themselves with some sweetcakes, and watermelons they had gathered in the field, then made for this hole. The Boers returned at noon; 16 of them, all mounted, with spare horses carrying ammunition. The Boers came riding carelessly along their spoor, but our fellows sat tight until their leader, when within 40 yards of the hole, saw them and said: 'Hier's de Kaffers.'[35] A man hit him on the breast and knocked him down. He fired, while [he] was on the ground, wounding one of our chaps on the buttocks before another hit him on the forehead.

After this our fellows had a brief but very hot battle. The Boers ran away leaving six dead men and five horses on the field. Two horses were taken alive, with their saddles, bridles, etc., by our fellows; also two rifles and bandoliers belonging to the dead Boers.

From here our men came homeward. They put the wounded man on one of the horses and came all along the railway line. The Boers accompanied them from a distance of between 800 and 1 000 yards, sniping at them all the time. They continued this until they reached Ga-Koi-Koi (four miles from here) then thought it advisable to go back again as it was too early to come into Mafeking. They did so and the Boers accompanied them back again to Madibe where they waited until it was late enough to cross the Boer lines and get into Mafeking under cover of the dark. When they left Madibe the Boers left them for good and went to fetch their dead. Their horses are a beautiful grey gelding with a first-class saddle, and a big mare. The bridles and other saddle are third-hand. The two rifles are a splendid pair of Martini's 'Made especially for the Z.A.R. by Wesley Richards.' This was stamped very neatly: 'J. J. Jonck, Z.A.R. 1900' within a circle.

Our losses were: one man, wounded at the fight, and one man wounded slightly during the march, at long range. The enemy's losses were one man and his horse, killed at the koppie, six Boers and three horses, killed during the fight, one man and one horse killed while our fellows were coming down along the hill, and two horses taken away alive. We wonder how many wounded.

'Au Sanna' is very hot now, like yesterday. She gave us thunder and lightning all day. She, however, did no damage during the day, but her last shell this evening did considerable damage and also struck a place that had never been struck before – the court house. At 5.00 p.m. there are always a number of people congregated in the yard to fall in for their night's duty, get pay, etc., etc. The soup kitchen is close by and as soup is issued in the afternoon there are hundreds of Natives always gathered there. The shell came round at 6.15, flew over the roof and abruptly dropped over the chimney into what at one time was the C.C. and R.M.'s[36] private office, and made a terrible wreck of everything inside: the partitions, walls, chairs, books, tables, etc.; but the greatest of all mysteries is how the shell went [on] to bag the people outside, amputated legs, shattered bodies and heads to the number of eight killed and wounded – a doleful procedure.

Wednesday, 14th

'Au Sanna' is still as hot as ever. We have heard this morning about 'relief of Ladysmith' in duplicated despatches from the north. The originals have been caught by the Boers evidently, for bearers state that the runners who preceded them have been caught.

A lot of women are always going out to their fields at Moleloane to gather melons and fresh kaffircorn. They go right across the Boer lines. There are so few Boers in the trenches that they cannot control the multitude of women. If they tell 16 to drop their stuff 'about 60' will bring in theirs from somewhere else. This shows that the Boer trenches are quite empty and 're tshosiwa ka merora fela'.[37] They have all gone north to oppose Plumer. That is why Natives[38] are guarding now.

Thursday, 15th

It rained during last night. We have rain nearly every day. Teacher Kolobe came back. His following of five supported him right through. They attacked a Boer homestead on Tuesday but failed to bag the cattle as the farmers were too numerous for them. They came back via Madibe and saw the dead and wounded horses shot by the balance of his party on Monday.

They killed one Boer in the attempt to capture cattle.

I had a very narrow escape at 4 o'clock this afternoon. My first warning was but the screeching of the shell when it came straight up to me. I was riding 'Pony' round from Lookoane and turning round the curve at Letsi's[39] place. I hardly knew what to do as for six seconds (or thereabouts) I felt that it was coming straight to me. I have never felt so nasty as during that little period of my life, until it burst and the pieces flew overhead. The pony had already turned round and was going backwards with me.

The result was a bloodstirring whine amongst the womenfolk in the house next to me. I myself was so shaken that I scarcely felt anything when I heard that it had smashed old Letsi's head and killed the poor old fellow instantly.

These narrow escapades are not only undesirable because one barely escapes death, but surely because they give one the impression that many of them are in store for one in the little future left for one; and every one of them will be narrower than its predecessor – until he loses a leg, arm, some limb, or even life.

Many people are leaving Mafeking at night now. They experience no difficulty in crossing the outpost and the Boer lines. We are all convinced that the Boers have considerably diminished during the past week or two.

We are very restless about the safety of the two parties of cattle raiders still at large.

I heard something very extraordinary today. The administrators of martial law have authorized the municipality to levy dog tax as they want to get rid of as many dogs as possible.[40] Some unlicensed dogs were found, destroyed and buried by the town ranger.

Our local Zambesi friends unearthed them, immediately the ranger's assistants left the scene, and promptly cooked them for dinner, which gave the Barolong sections of the community the impression that there is more in a dog than they were ever told there was.

Friday, 16th

It was not so hot as we have had it from 'Sanna' since the beginning of the week.

McKenzie has taken Jackal Tree with his 'Black Watch' of which Titshalakazi's 'Gun'[41] was a member when he got shot. They went to Jackal Tree at the beginning of the week and found no Boers there. He occupied the place but vacated it on account of it being so far away from here, and far away from any water. Last night, however, they went up there and took shelter in the Boer trench. They saw them coming: one Boer and three Natives (rebels), all mounted. They came, off-saddled their horses, and laid down their rifles when our Transkeian friends coolly volleyed them, killing the Boer and a rebel, wounding one rebel, and causing the other to run away. They took their four horses with saddles, rifles, etc.

We are anxiously waiting for runners and we wonder why we receive no news.

Saturday, 17th

We are feeling the strain a little, not because we are defeated but simply because we have received no despatches this week.

There are some Shangaans and Zambesis – very few of them, as the majority have left this place and gone up country. They are going to be fed on soup, the 'stuff' we hear was used for white ladies in Kimberley. Here it is used by destitute people who cannot provide for themselves. It was not really a case of starvation but planned strategy on the part of the officers.[42]

Sunday, 18th

A funny thing – we received no fewer than eight runners today, all from the south. One left here early in December. His mate returned in the road. One left here late in December; his mate got sick and he left him half-way. Two left here in January and they were four when they left Kimberley on the 18th *ult*. Two were sent to Setlagoli by Lady Sarah Wilson. They managed to deliver their messages in what may be termed a 'Sherlock Holmeish' sort of fashion. From there they went to Motlotli Emang's:[43] they got there simply through the doings of providence. One afternoon, being sick, they called on what they found to be a wayside farmhouse for hospitality. On stating that they came from Mafeking the previous week and were requesting to be concealed against Boer discovery, they were told to go inside. They saw the children running to the fields to report to the lady what important visitors there were at the house. She came – Motlotli Emang did – sat down, gasped, sighed, then muttered in broken sentences: 'So you are from Mafeking?'

'Yes.'

'Do you know anybody named Plaatje?'

'Oh yes, he is . . .'

'Is he still alive and well?'

'Yes, he is in charge of our work and if you treat us hospitably you would be obliging him.'

She heaved a big sigh of relief, then went outside, they believe, to weep with joy, for on her return she said that she had always heard that three-quarters of the inhabitants of Mafeking had been killed by 'Sanna' and she was always thinking I was one of them.

Two of the runners are Mr Weil's. They left here in February for Kimberley. They were taken prisoners at Maribogo[44] and sent down to Vryburg, where they were kept as prisoners-at-large for some time. During that time they heard that Mr Rosenblatt was sending despatches between Vryburg and Kimberley and handed the despatches to him. They were buried in a furrow outside the town all this time. All of these runners have been picking each other up on the road, and just outside Mafeking they came across one party of cattle-raiders and they all came in. The fellows from Kimberley say that they never expected that Kimberley would hold out up to the end.

The condition of the inhabitants was very miserable. They had no words to describe the state of the people. White ladies fleeing, babies in hand and piccaninnies all round, to the bottom of the mine[45] – tens of fathoms deep, to take cover from the shells. They never for a moment thought that the people would hold out, and they often told them that Mafeking was not half as badly off as that.

When the troops arrived it was something worth seeing. They say that we who were not there missed a very touching scene. White ladies can scream, they say, just as loud as Native women – 'Ya ba retla tlhoyana'.[46] They said they saw thousands of Boers being marched to gaol and they were surprised. They wondered how so many people could surrender to other warriors when they had their guns, ammunition and everything. They have a far greater contempt for the Boers than they ever thought they would have. Fancy surrendering to other men when you are armed. The Serolong axiom for an armed man is: 'Shoa o ikaletse',[47] i.e. even if your antagonists be a hundred, kill at least one before they catch you.

They came past Pniel.[48] Rev. Westphal has been taken prisoner along with four men – one of them I think is Abel Pienaar.[49] The three are Bechuanas and goodness knows who they are. Barkly[50] has been retaken. The Boers all fled from there like wild rabbits immediately at the sight of the British. It is marvellous how Rev. Westphal managed to turn traitor,[51] when he sent me that hot letter going for me for having leanings towards the Transvaal and

Krugerism, simply because I sympathized with Adv. Burton[52] during the last election; and he could not be convinced by my reasons that the young Q.C. earned my sympathies not because he was supported by the Afrikander Bond, but simply because he was a negrophilist and did a lot for us while I was in Kimberley. He acted on our behalf directly on the platform, in the press, and at the bar.[53]

The effects of the war are going to be bitterer still – no matter what its results. But this is one of those things, as Lord Dundreary would say, 'No fellah can understand.'

They brought much news about the doings of the Boers outside today. The little skirmishes our people had with the Boers outside have had a great effect among the latter. It is reported that about 1 000 armed Barolongs are scattered all over the country. Two hundred of them are at Madibi and they have two Maxims. Mathakgong's name is a household word on every farm. The cattle have been centralized and strong guards put over them. They are strongly encamped in trenches surrounding the cattle fence, and they are just ready to give him a cordial reception. They say he has killed many Boers at their farms during last month, including women and children.

They have been informed that the Kromdraai laager was going to be moved to the border last Friday. Goodness knows if it is true. But we wonder how the Boers can stay around here much longer when they had such a good knock at Kimberley and the troops[54] were at the Vaal on the 20th of last month.

Tuesday, 20th

I have been very busy officially – so busy that I have failed to jot down a note or two, and I scarcely remember what took place yesterday beyond a few notes that I consider worth recording. While at court this morning I was practising shorthand and I find the following:

> Albert pleaded not guilty to being found on the premises of Masethaisho without permission at about midnight last Saturday. The evidence showed that the complainant is a young widow and resides by herself with a little child in the hut.
>
> An old man was called upon to give evidence. After being duly sworn, he denied all knowledge of the case. Asked what he came to town for, he answered: 'Merely for a stroll.' (The court was held in the open air.)
>
> Case no. 2 was an old Zulu charged with stealing some wood

from the Government 'scherm'[55] between the hospital and convent. Plea: 'Not guilty', as he did not know that the wood was anyone's property.

Case no. 3: 'Some-one-or-other' – theft of green mealies, the property of Samson Gape.[56]

Case no. 4: An old, miserable-looking, half-starved Changaan[57] was charged with theft of green mealies – the property of the chief, Lekoko. The plea: 'Guilty, under provocation – hunger.'

Case no. 5: Lucas, a Bosoanalander,[58] suspected as a spy. The prisoner, without being called upon to plead, was remanded.

Case no. 6: Willie Maretletle of B.P.,[59] a special guard at the gaol, pleaded not guilty to neglect of duty in that he did, on or about the 18th inst., wrongly and unlawfully permit prisoner 'Captain' to go into the gaol kitchen against orders.

Case no. 7: 'Captain', a prisoner undergoing a sentence of nine months with hard labour, pleaded not guilty to the theft of a pannikin of soup – prisoners' rations.

Case no. 1: guilty. The court came to the conclusion that the prisoners must have been aware that the complainant was a widow who lived by herself, and that they were there for a very serious purpose. The charge ought to have been that of attempted rape. Sentence – 36 lashes with the cat-o'-nine-tails.

Case no. 2: verdict – guilty. Sentence – that he be attached to De Kock's Corner for a period of three days, watching the 'scherm' against wood thieves.

Case no. 3: verdict – guilty. Sentence – six days with hard labour.

Case no. 4: verdict – guilty, but prisoner being too weak and 'maar'[60] to undergo sentence – is remanded *sine die*.

The big 94-pounder was on very splendid terms with me this morning. The 'loading and pointing' bells range early this morning but the gun never fired until I left home for town. I walked to Mr Stent's place in a very finicky mood, but just when I was within 20 yards of the door of his dug-out, the last bell rang; and I was just in time to take shelter. When I left Stent, the next waited till I crossed the Market Square and took shelter at Lippmann's. Shell no. 3 waited until I reached the chief pay-master's dug-out, and from there I went to the residency. I put the typewriter at the door of our little bomb-proof and was going to commence my work, when the bell rang again and I bobbed in. The usual row took place, there was a pause and then a loud 'xap' and bits of gravel drizzled into the dug-out. When we came out I thought my fatty little pony had followed Whiskey, for the table was simply enveloped in a cloud of dust. A short time revealed the fact that the well had been smashed; and the fact that the shell exploded right in the water is accountable for the unusually curt report of the explosion.

It rained during the afternoon. If we had as much food as rain, then things would be alright.

Wednesday, 21st

Myself, Philemon and Mr Gates are taking a census of the stadt. The latter and an assistant are taking it across the river. Phil starts at Tloung,[61] myself at Bokone, and we'll meet in the centre. It is a tedious, bothersome job. We commenced at 7.00 and at 10.00 I was knocked up. The people are vexing me exceedingly: one would ask me what I wished to do with the name of the owner of a place, another would object to a repetition of the census as they were counted (registered) twice already during the present siege. Another would say: 'No wonder the present, unlike all previous sieges of Mafeking, is so intolerable for the unfortunate beleaguered people are counted like sheep.' Another would stand at the door, empty herself of the whole of her stock of bad words, then threaten me to 'just touch my pen and jot down any numbers of her family'. The so-and-so!

Another would give a cordial reception – so cordial that I would fancy that she will offer me a pipe full or a cigarette. She will act to my greatest satisfaction throughout in every way, except giving me the proper answer. I never knew that my store of patience was so bottomless – until the evening when I came home and found I had no fewer than 1 677 persons on my list.

I have not been to town all day today – the first day for three months. I hear 5 miles[62] has been captured by the Cape Boys from the Boers at the brickfields. The Kromdraai laager is moved away from there. Two runners who were bound for Kimberley failed to leave owing to the long train of Boer waggons from Kromdraai circuiting round to the Transvaal side of the place – the first dawn of liberty.

Mathakgong left with nearly 30 men on another cattle-raiding expedition – his fourth during the present siege.

I have not seen my siege friends (the beggars) today. There were always scores of them every day at the residency and they were relieved by the soup kitchen. They are made up of the blackish races of this continent – mostly Zulus and Zambesians. They venerate the Civil Commissioner and call me 'ngwana's molimo'.[63] It is really pitiful to see one who was too unfortunate to hear soon enough that there was a residency in Mafeking, and, being too weak to work, never had a chance to steal anything during the last six days, and so had nothing to eat. Last month one died in the Civil Commissioner's yard. It was a miserable scene to be surrounded by about 50 hungry beings, agitating the engagement of your pity and to see one of them succumb to his agonies and fall backwards with a dead thud. Surely these Transvaal Boers are abominable. I really do not think they are children of the same Dutchland as the inhabitants of the O.F.S. No wonder their president was a judge while Oom Paul was a 'schaapwachter'.[64]

I wonder where is Gates: my total for today is 1 677, Philemon's 734. They were getting on much worse than I. Keshupile was his 'moshupatsela.'[65] He went with him till dinner-time and then started grumbling that he did not estimate that the trouble of this work was a tenth of what it is. Tshipithata[66] is away cattle raiding.

Thursday, 22nd

Turned out at 7.00 and tackled the census. I reached our home on the beat at 8.40 then paused a bit for breaking fast. After this I went on with it again, knocked off at 12.00 for lunch; at it again at 3.00 to 4.30, when I finished it all.

I had	2 597	There are therefore no fewer than
Mr Gates	1 557	5 448 people in the stadt.
Mr Mahlelebe	1 294	

This shows that about 10 000 people were in the stadt at the commencement of hostilities, as quite half the population have been clearing out in four's and five's as the tension became more and more strained.

Friday, 23rd

We had another very quiet day. There must be some sort of a machinery resolving itself in a way decidedly unpleasant to the Boers. They have not fired a shot with their big gun – the first time for two days in succession. The runners who were caught came in this morning with good news.

Saturday, 24th

Morning dawned somewhat pleasantly. During the night the Boers were forced to leave their trenches in the brickfields – the nearest to Mafeking – and fall 1 000 yards backwards. When

our forces occupied the Dutch 'marope'[67] they suddenly remembered that the place is most certainly mined with dynamite and
immediately searched and discovered the spot where the mine
is, then cut the chord which the enemy was going to pull in order
to cause a destructive explosion. This must have caused the Boers
to wonder why the thing refused to work – but such was the case.
The mine was emptied and the dynamite brought into town.

Fresh newspapers were found in the trench stating Bloemfontein
had been occupied last month, and other valuable information.
Also that three cattle-raiders were caught stealing 38 head of
cattle on the 17th – they were all killed and the cattle recaptured
minus casualties – and similar 'rot'.

The laager at Kromdraai is moving round. We hope all the
waggons have passed today. Runners said Col. Plumer was at
Macheng[68] the day before yesterday, making for Disaneng[69] with
500 men. Our raiders came in with some cattle and good news.
We will soon be cheering. The big gun never fired again today
and things looked quite pleasant. We had a sweet holiday.
Tshipithata.[70]

Sunday, 25th
No change yet is apparent. We had a very windy day, which
made the Sunday somewhat unpleasant. Emang has been such
an acquisition to our domestic circle that we wonder what we can
do without her. It was, besides, a boon to her as it made her
unused to the ceremonious 'squatting' and allowed her to occupy
her time in cooking and doing such household practice as will fit
her for greater cares in future. She already knows not only how to
cook, but also how to economize with the scanty groceries and
preserves everything with skill and forethought. She takes more
pride in keeping the room and furniture tidy than in joining
useless games in 'nooks and corners'[71] as Rev. Msikinya would
say; but still, for all, Mafikeng gives me notice that I must be
prepared to part with her on Wednesday next. This is the worst
news I have received for months. I was unable to speak to her, as
I considered she took a pride in seeing her daughter learning so
progressively, and the question took me by very great surprise.

We get our rations – groceries (tea, coffee, sugar, pepper, and
salt), vegetables (green mealies, beet, cabbage, turnips, carrots,
etc., from the gardens and fields on the river beds) and preserved
meat – from a government store provided for the purpose. These
we draw weekly and have to call early for them, once every week,

but the bread is a nuisance for this we have to call for once every day, and each time one gets a little bit – not fit to keep St Leger alive more than a few hours. If the issuer likes, he can successfully cause us to do without it by telling our messenger that he was too late if he called at 7.00 in the morning and too early if he called at 3.00 in the afternoon; and when he comes at the right time, he would tell the messenger that I should have called personally, well knowing that this is an impossibility.

Monday, 26th

We had a very quiet day, there being hardly anything worth mentioning except in the afternoon, when a 7-pounder was posted in the brickfields and shelled the Boer trenches. This drew all the wrath of 'Au Sanna' on the brickfields and she went for the bricks with all the vigour and strength she can command. It was quite a novelty to hear her after the last five days of peacefulness. There was no danger on either side.

Tuesday, 27th

I woke at 5.00 to find a fine peaceful morning. One could even wish that a morning like that ought to find one in a peaceful neighbourhood where one will partake of the sweet balmy air without any interference. I found I had nothing to do, so I lay down to slumber again. Just a little after 6.00 again the 9-pounder Krupp opened the ball from Game Tree. I was wondering at it when it was followed by what appeared to be a 15-pounder from Jackal Tree, by 'Au Sanna', and several others. They kept it up all the morning. Every bomb-proof in the place was almost useless as shells were bursting from every direction.

It was a terrible morning.[72] When I left home I was simply bewildered and hardly knew what to do. I was intending to go up to the rocks, which I had deserted since the middle of November, for since then we never had it half so hot. Even at New Year it was terrible; but nothing resembling this. I stopped at the rocks, which are much more comfortable than a dug-out, where one cannot see what goes on outside. I was wondering if this was going to be our future lot, or whether it was simply a one day's warming up. It is difficult to describe the scene, just as difficult as it is to tell how many guns there were against us. We are only sure of one thing, and that is that there were some big guns against us which have not been in Mafeking [before]. Since the big gun left its first position our house has always been out of its view so that it has not been in danger of being hit, but this morning they were mercilessly in our line. A fragment of shell that burst just at the Gape's dropped on the roof of the back house, but did not penetrate it. While I was going to the rocks, 'Au Sanna' was firing in such rapid succession that three shells burst all about me before I got there. This is to say nothing at least of the smaller fry. I screwed up as much courage as I could and left the rocks to go to the Court of S.J.[73] in town. It was something unbearable while I was walking between the town and the stadt to see a horse being blown to smithereens; but when I reached the town I met the prisoners being marched back to gaol – the court was already over.

The by-word, of course, was 'what could be the meaning of this heavy entertainment?' It was something invigorating for me to find a man who had come from Kimberley with despatches and had left the troops in Vryburg.[74] This is such good news that one does not mind the heavy shelling; but still things are just as mixed-up as they could be. A 12-pound shell went in through the air pipe of a dug-out, in which a lady and her family were sheltered, bursting inside, injuring the lady and wounding her servant girl. Sergt. Abrams, the white Morolong, got the front half of his foot knocked off while he was in the stadt visiting a Native whose buttocks had been knocked clean off by a shell. One woman had her jaws dislocated and shattered.

I took a statement from the man who saw the troops, then lost my shorthand notes, and failed to remember what he had told me and the public did not read it till the following day.[75] Nine horses were killed that day and I wonder how many more animals. By dinner time 'Au Sanna' alone had put in 65 shells – i.e. 6 110 pounds of cast iron, mortar, etc., into the place – a record in 1900.

There was a brief respite at 12.00 noon during which I rode home, but it only gave me a chance to reach there. I have been subjected to shellfire every day for five months, during which the Boers always had a great reverence for breakfast and dinner hours, but today they treated these two hours with very great disrespect.

We are all very sorry at Sergt. Abrams being wounded at this time. He was the father of the Barolong snipers and a very brave man. Three Natives wounded at the soup kitchen concluded the day's damage to life and property. The man who tells us about the troops states that Bud, and several others, reached Kimberley after its relief. This is such cheerful news that one's head can hardly hold the joy; but I could nearly knock him down for not having told him that he was intending to come up here.[76] It took me some time to realize the fact that when we despatch runners we would object to their preaching [their] intended journey from every housetop.

Wednesday, 28th

We had a very quiet day. Still and peaceful, next to no shooting. During the morning I rode over to the location to purchase one of the horses lifted from the Boers by the Fingoes. I met the fellow in town and [he] told me that I could have the gelding for £14.10.0. I told Rajane[77] to get a note from him, and take it over to the seller's brother who would receive the money from him, and hand over the horse. Subsequently, I rode over to the location myself, and found the 'brother'(?) who, even if he had been inclined to hand over any horse, appeared to have no horse at all. I asked him to fetch it, but he said he wondered where it was. When I explained the puerility of allowing a horse to stray out of view, particularly when it is a captured horse which is likely to bolt away any minute, he appeared very seedy, but volunteered to walk about the location looking for the horse with me. He, however, succeeded to polish me off by telling me that the sellers had gone to town on horseback. I demanded Rajane's note and to my utter amazement, found the wording to be as follows: 'Lendoda ifunaku tenga ihashe nge £15 kodwa u linde mna nodofika.'[78]

Shortly after this, I learnt that the horse was sold at 9 o'clock this morning. I, however, waited until the cheat's arrival and on demanding my horse, he knocked about the location from house to house inquiring if the people had not seen this horse. One little boy curtly gave him the following answer: 'Kaloku waya nalo edolopene andikange ndilibone.'[79] This fairly knocked him up and he nearly fell on his knees begging me to go home as he was sure to bring the horse at 3.30 p.m. It is 11.10 already, and no horse has turned up yet – the long and short of it was that when the spoil was divided he preferred to retain the horse. He was only entitled to £7, and, as the horse was valued at £12, he had to refund £5. The owners of the £5 were pressing him for the money, so he sold the horse this morning. The reason why he wanted to sell it over again to me may be found in exactly the same spot – that of the cause of the suit: 'Dingiswayo vs Moss'.[80] By the way, he is also a Dingiswayo.

During the afternoon I purchased a spank from Lt. McKenzie, 'Black Watch', at £16 and I immediately got a job for him.

Rajane is anxious to ride despatches, and he is such a professional horseman that he won't do it on foot. No horse has, as yet, left and come into Mafeking since the end of October last year, and this is rather a perilous adventure. He took my new charger and a few packets of letters, and started for Vryburg. I accompanied him up to the outside forts, which are just within a stone's throw of the Boer lines, to listen if they would fire at him. So I left here with him at 7.00 o'clock. We rode and rode to the south of the stadt, but could not find any forts. Jacob[81] told me that we had passed them, and were already within disputed territory, but I thought he was merely fooling. He even told me that he would rather tell me to return and go on himself, but he cannot do so as he must see the advanced guards for guidance, so we came back homeward, much against my will.

We came along a broad road and to our surprise, after riding a long distance, we observed a fort in front of us – we had passed it about half-a-mile [back]. When we got there the fellows were all game, and imagining that we were Boers, had their rifles ready cocked – about six or seven on each of us. They waited until we were within ten yards of the fort, then challenged us. They recognized our voices and came out to meet us. They sent us to 'Teacher's fort'[82] with a guide and there Rajane received his final injunctions and left us at 3.50. I remained there listening attentively for any fire that could be heard at Jacob. He was only 15 minutes away when the fellows all said he was through, but I strained and listened for another 70 minutes – when I was cocksure of his safe departure. By the time I left they were all confident that he had already passed Madibe.

During the time I spent at the fort there was a discussion as to whether he[83] is going to accelerate or relax the progress of the troops, and the debate turned in favour of the latter thought. Rajane is a brave man, no mistake! He was the first D.R.[84] who ever left Mafeking, on October 14th. After this, matters became so serious that no horse could cross the Boers round Mafeking for over four months, and he again is the first to venture out on horseback.

Thursday, 29th

Another very quiet day. 'Au Sanna' never fired a shot today. Emang has left our mess in obedience to maternal instruction.

Today, before the summary jurisdiction court, a Shangaan was charged with the theft of a horse. The prisoner pleaded something equivalent to 'guilty under provocation'. He had been living on 'thepe'.[85] This is partly wholesome as long as it is green, but it becomes bitter and indigestible as soon as the sun's rays affect it. We have not had rain for ten days; and the heat is so intense that five days without rain dries the grass completely and our friend's plea was therefore justifiable. The man could have been convicted if it were not for Col. Hore. He always views things in the same light, and often makes as sarcastic remarks as the supreme court judges. When his brother justice was about to find the man guilty, he said: 'The soup-kitchen people are to blame for these shameful deeds. Just look at him: his two legs are scarcely able to hold the fellow's body. They don't feed the people at all.'

He wouldn't agree to any verdict and it was decided his case would wait until the soup-kitchen affair had been investigated.

Mr Bell issues free tickets to people without means and they always come to say that they do not get any soup although they had the ticket.

Old Tshipithata simply died suddenly this morning. He was a bit sickly and the illness increased during last week when he was out cattle raiding.

Friday, 30th

We are having abnormally quiet days lately.

The Colonel Commanding has published a hot protest against alleged rumours by somebodies,[86] to the effect that he delays the troops and that he starves the inhabitants, etc., in the *Mafeking Mail*. He threatens to catch those fellows when their claims [prove false].[87]

THE COLONEL ON 'GROUSING'

I hear that again wiseacres are busy in town, informing people as to what I am doing and what I am leaving undone. As their deductions are somewhat inaccurate I wish to state that the condition of affairs is in no way altered since my last general notice, which stated we must be prepared to remain besieged all that time. Indeed I hope that we may be free within the next fortnight or three weeks, but it would be folly on our part not to be prepared against possible unforeseen delays. Had we not been thus prepared in the first instance we should all have been prisoners in Pretoria by the beginning of January, and the Boers would now have been enjoying the use of our property in Mafeking.

I am, I suppose, the most anxious of anybody in Mafeking to see a relief column here and the siege at an end; all that can be done for our relief, from both north and south, is being done, but the moves of troops in the face of the enemy must necessarily be slow, and we have to sit in patience until they develop.

As regards the smallness of our rations, we could, of course, live well on full rations for a week or two and then give in to the 'women slaughterers' and let them take their vengeance on the town, whereas by limiting our amount of daily food we can make certain of outlasting all their efforts against us. The present ration, properly utilised, is a fairly full one as compared with those issued in other sieges – in fact I and my staff have, during the past few days, been living on a far smaller ration without any kind of extras to improve it – and we still live.

There are, by the way, two hints I should like to give for making small rations go further – hints derived from personal experience of previous hungry times – and these are:

1. To lump your rations together as much as possible for cooking, and not every man to have his little amount cooked separately.

2. To make the whole into a big thick stew, from which, even three quarter lbs. of ingredients per man, three good meals can be got per day.

It is just possible that we may have to take 2 ozs. off the bread stuffs, but otherwise our supplies will last well over the period indicated. It has been objected that we are feeding horses on oats, but the oats so used are a lot (of colonial oats) that have been found quite useless for making flour from for human consumption.

I am told that I keep back news from the public. This is not in accordance with facts, for I make a point of publishing all news of general interest as soon as possible after receipt, first by telephone, then by notices posted about, and lastly through Mr Whales, in the *Mafeking Mail* slips; I have no object whatever in keeping news back. Occasionally, of course, items of military information have to be kept quiet because, as we all know, their publication in Mafeking means their transmission within a few hours, to the enemy's camp.

Although it may have been somewhat out of my province, I have been writing to the High Commissioner as strongly as I could put them, the claims which the citizens and refugees have for consideration in the matter of compensation, pressing for very early settlement on some more satisfactory basis than was the case on a former occasion. And there is no doubt that the good part they have borne in the defence of the place will add great force to their claims.

I have no feeling of doubt whatever that the large majority of the townspeople have sufficient confidence in me to know that I am working, as far as possible, for their good, but there are always busybodies in every assemblage to cavil at whatever is done, and I should just like to remind these gentlemen of the order issued early in the siege about 'grousing'.

I am always not only willing but anxious to personally hear any reasonable complaints or suggestions, and those who have them to make, need only bring their grievances to me to get what redress is in my power, but veiled hints and growlings cannot be permitted; at such times as these they are apt to put people 'on edge' and to alarm the ladies, and for these reasons they must be suppressed. 'Grousing' is generally the outcome of funk on the part of the individual who grouses, and I hope that every right-minded man who hears any of it will shut it up with an appropriate remark, or the toe of his boot. Cavillers should keep quiet until the siege is over and then they are welcome to write or talk until they are blue in the face.

By these remarks I do not wish for one instant to suggest that this 'grousing' is widespread. On the contrary the patience and loyal obedience of the main body of the inhabitants under the restrictions of martial law, form one of the conspicuous features of the siege. But there are a few individual grumblers – most of whom are known to me (as they will find when their claims for compensation come up for adjudication) – and it is these gentlemen that I desire to warn to keep quiet as otherwise I shall have to take more stringent steps against them, but I should be ashamed if the fame of Mafeking and its heroic defence should be marred by any whisper among envious outsiders, that there was any want of harmony or unity of purpose among us.

R. S. S. BADEN-POWELL,
Colonel.

EDITORIAL NOTE

The entry for Friday 30th March is the last of Plaatje's diary, although the siege itself was to continue for several more weeks. Since there were over 20 sheets of blank paper remaining in the notebook in which the diary was written it seems very unlikely that the remainder of the diary was completed but subsequently lost. Rather, the likelihood is that pressure of work compelled Plaatje to first of all fall behind with his entries, which certainly happened during the last few weeks he wrote it, and then to cease them entirely. The general sense of pessimism that prevailed in Mafeking in the latter part of March and early April probably also contributed to this decision.

In the stadt the threat of starvation had become an urgent issue. Here it was no longer a matter of discomfort, but of life or death. The cause of these desperate Barolong was taken up by certain of the townspeople who felt that the African food situation demanded a moral decision. But this campaign failed, as the military authorities stood firmly behind the prevailing arrangements. Apologists for Baden-Powell (of whom Grinnell-Milne is perhaps the most ardent) claim that the 'obvious answer' was that the garrison would have been 'starved into surrender within two weeks' – and that, in the hands of the Boers, the Barolong would not have fared well.[88] The validity of this speculation, is, however, questionable.

It is not only in respect of the 'Native Question' that the Commanding Officer was, for the first time, being criticized. There were persistent rumours that Baden-Powell wished to prolong the siege, thereby causing unnecessary hardship to the population. The threat to morale that this gossip was posing prompted Baden-Powell's letter of denial at the end of the month. Also, the garrison emphasized that, on the military front, significant progress was being made. The capture of trenches in the brickfields and successes in the artillery duels were enthusiastically reported in the *Mafeking Mail*.

As Plaatje's entries for this month reflect, there was a widespread belief within the lines of investment that relief was imminent. This is perhaps why the criticism and the gossip gained no real ground among the civilians. But relief was, in fact, almost six weeks off, and during this final period the people of Mafeking were to be tested more seriously than they had been before.

Epilogue

A review of the day-to-day reports compiled during the siege conveys the impression that the first 23 days in April were, in most respects, unremarkable. There was little fighting of any description, though shelling reached a climax on the eleventh. After that day 'Au Sanna' fired no more, as the gun was transferred to Pretoria. Only the briefest of skirmishes punctuated the endurance test which the siege had become. Ammunition in Mafeking was in short supply, and the garrison had no desire to waste it on fruitless artillery duels. Furthermore, Baden-Powell received a communication from Lord Roberts on the 20th stating that the town would not be relieved by the 18 May, as had been intended. The food situation was, of course, serious, although locusts provided yet another source – especially for the Barolong in the stadt. The month of April, as recounted in the *Mafeking Mail*, was one of minor events arranged by the military leadership to allay the anxieties of the citizenry.

The 24th, however, marked the start of a new phase in the confrontation. On that day Sarel Eloff, the grandson of Paul Kruger, returned to Mafeking from Pretoria with reinforcements and a firm resolve to breach the six-month-old defences. The garrison prepared itself for an attack immediately after his arrival; but the previous pattern of intermittent shelling continued for a while, and May had a relatively quiet beginning.

The Sunday truce, which had been effectively honoured by both sides despite the odd misunderstanding and occasional threats, was broken on the first sabbath of the month. Heavy shelling provided a cover for a Boer raiding-party which successfully made off with a number of horses. Again the garrison expected an attack; and again nothing happened – at least, not for six days. On the 12th, Eloff mounted what turned out to be the final attempt to overrun Mafeking by direct onslaught.

Before dawn the town received intense fire from the east. While the garrison readied itself for the assault, and tried to anticipate the source from which it would come, Eloff and his

135

250 men crept quietly along the Molopo in the direction of the stadt. Guided by a British deserter who was familiar with the perimeter defences and their weaknesses, the Boer party intended to force its way into the town. As soon as this had been accomplished, reinforcements led by Snyman were to have completed the defeat of Mafeking. Eloff sent word to a Reuters correspondent that, at a given signal from the stadt, he should publish the news of the 'fall'.

Under cover of darkness they advanced stealthily into the maze of huts. Once Eloff had led his men away from the river and began to make for the British South African Police camp, he signalled his triumph. The thatched roof of a homestead was ignited and spectacular flames heralded the start of a lively battle. Soon the conflagration spread and a chaotic stampede to safety on the part of the Barolong obscured – and hence facilitated – the execution of a pincer movement toward the camp. In the meantime, the main Boer force abetted the advance with rifle-fire; but the offensive which General Snyman had promised to lead never materialized.

Eloff reached the B.S.A.P. camp and found it manned by sixteen soldiers of the Protectorate Regiment under Colonel Hore. The attacking party imprisoned these soldiers in the fort at its centre and proceeded to assume positions in the outbuildings. But, in the absence of support, the Boers soon found themselves isolated. One French volunteer who had accompanied Eloff climbed onto the roof of the fort with a bottle of Burgundy from the captured officers' mess and drank a toast to 'Fashoda'. He received only satirical comment from the surrounding British – and a sniper's bullet through the heart. The garrison had organized itself very rapidly and effected an 'investment-within-an-investment' with parade-ground precision. The stragglers that Eloff left behind him in the stadt were either killed or compelled to beat a hasty retreat to their own lines.

Throughout the day the young Boer commander held the fort against considerable odds. But, in the absence of water – the supply tank had been destroyed by rifle-fire – and reinforcement, many of his men chose to attempt an escape into the protective trees of the Molopo. By six o'clock in the evening Eloff was left no choice but to surrender to Colonel Hore. After a cease-fire had been arranged, Baden-Powell met the prisoners at the Market Square. Eloff had been convinced of his ability to take Mafeking in the half-light of dawn. 'Breakfast at Dixon's' had been his

rallying cry. He had arrived under slightly different circumstances –
for dinner. The officers of the beleaguered garrison were unan-
imous in the view that, despite his ultimate failure, the young
officer had earned the meal with his display of courage.

The 'fall of Mafeking' was reported as arranged and caused
predictable feelings of joy and despair. In fact, the truth differed
radically from the intelligence contained in the Reuters correspondent's despatch. On 16 May Colonel Mahon's relief force
from the south met Plumer approximately nineteen miles outside
Mafeking. Fighting their way through, the combined party reached
the outskirts of the town and paused to rest before effecting the
relief before dawn the next day. They met little opposition from
Snyman's weary soldiers and marched triumphantly into the
Market Square on the 17th of the month.

* * * *

So ended the siege of Mafeking. The daily rigours of the previous
weeks gave way to ceremony and celebration. Baden-Powell and
many members of the garrison left for new theatres of war.
Citizens who had been evacuated to safety in October began to
arrive back by the restored rail service, and community life in the
town slowly returned to normal. Those who had persisted in
keeping diaries throughout the long months of investment drew
them to a close. 'We are now relieved and breathe the air of
freedom once more,' wrote Charles Bell, concluding his journal.
'The whole country is singing our praises, and Mafeking has
made a name for itself, which will be recorded in history.
Although we have suffered many hardships and troubles, we
nevertheless all feel proud to think that each individual, both
European and Native, has done his utmost to maintain the
honour of the British Empire.' There is no reason to believe that
Plaatje, who typed these words for Bell on the office typewriter,
would not have associated himself fully with the sentiments
expressed by them.

In the stadt, the Barolong listened to tributes paid to their
bravery and resilience, and were assured of continued political
protection from the Boers. In return, they formally pledged their
'unswerving loyalty' to Her Majesty and the Imperial Government.
But they were later to feel more than a little dissatisfied with
British breach of promise. The 'foreign' Africans of the Black
Watch and other contingents were to be given a farm as a collective

reward for their part in the defence. They, too, never received it. The saddest irony of all, however, lay in the events of 12 January, 1902. That night, Boer forces from the Transvaal crossed into the stadt, inflicted great damage to property, and carried off vast numbers of cattle and other livestock. The Barolong were in no position to resist. They had been disarmed by the British military authorities shortly after Mafeking was relieved, despite their strong protests, and could now only watch helplessly as the attackers wreaked havoc. More animals were lost and more damage suffered in that one night than during the entire seven months of siege.

At a personal level, Plaatje could look back upon the siege with every satisfacton. He had gained a wealth of experience which was to prove invaluable in his future career as a journalist, and his work had been of recognized value to the authorities. Charles Bell declared himself well pleased with his 'faithful interpreter, Solomon T. Plaatje,' and commended the reports he drew up on 'the Native situation': 'his style,' said Bell, 'though naive in manner, conveys accurately what the Native meant and is a record, of what happened, from a Native point of view.' Plaatje himself was not unaware of the worth of these reports. 'This arrangement was so satisfactory,' he noted later, 'that Mr Bell was created a C.M.G. at the end of the siege.'

During the weeks after the relief of Mafeking Plaatje was kept busy in the office, processing compensation claims and helping to collect evidence for the prosecution of those subjects of the Cape Colony who had taken up arms against the Imperial Government. Early in June, he wrote a long letter to Charles Bell to request an increase in salary, reminding him of the satisfactory services he had always endeavoured to provide, 'especially during the trying times we both had to undergo for upwards of six months of the siege'. He was awarded an increase of twelve pounds a year.

In December 1900, Plaatje travelled to Cape Town to write the civil service examinations which he had intended to do the previous year. He took the papers in Dutch and Typewriting, and came first among all candidates, black and white, in each subject; undoubtedly, the experience he had obtained during the siege helped him to achieve such high levels of proficiency. But the Cape Civil Service was never likely to offer a satisfactory career for a young man of Plaatje's ambitions and talents.

In 1901 he became involved, with Silas Molema, in setting up a

Setswana language newspaper in Mafeking, hoping thereby to provide a forum for the expression of African views, and to ensure that black interests would be taken into account in the post-war settlement yet to come. Some months later, it was agreed that he would become the editor of an enlarged version of this newspaper, *Koranta ea Becoana* ('The Bechuana Gazette'), and that it would be published in English as well as the vernacular. On 27 March 1902, Plaatje handed in his letter of resignation from the Civil Service, and began to devote all his time to the new venture. It was the start of a long and distinguished public career.

Bibliography

Agar-Hamilton, J. A. I., *The Road to the North. South Africa 1852–1886* (London: Longmans, 1937).

Baillie, Major F. D., *Mafeking: a Diary of the Siege* (London: Constable, 1900).

Bell, C. G. H., 'Diary during the Siege of Mafeking' (unpublished manuscript, MS 7348, Cory Library, Rhodes University, Grahamstown).

Breutz, P. -L., *The Tribes of the Mafeking District*, Department of Native Affairs Ethnological Publication no. 32 (Pretoria, 1956).

—, P.-L., *The Tribes of the Marico District*, Department of Native Affairs Ethnological Publication no. 30 (Pretoria, 1953).

Cowan, V., 'Diary of the Siege of Mafeking' (unpublished manuscript, Mafeking Museum).

Gardiner, B., *Mafeking: a Victorian Legend* (London: Cassell, 1966).

Grinnell-Milne, D., *Baden-Powell at Mafeking* (London: Bodley Head, 1957).

Hamilton, J. A., *The Siege of Mafeking* (London: Methuen, 1900).

Kuper, A., *Kalahari Village Politics: an African Democracy*, Cambridge Studies in Social Anthropology no. 3 (London: Cambridge University Press, 1970).

Mackenzie, J., *Austral Africa: Losing It or Ruling It* (London: Sampson Low, 1887).

Matthews, Z. K., 'A Short History of the Tshidi-Barolong', in *Fort Hare Papers*, vol. I, no. 1 (1945).

Molema, S. M., *The Bantu Past and Present* (Cape Town: Struik, 1963). This is a facsimile reprint of the 1920 edition published in Edinburgh by Green & Son.

—, *Montshiwa: Barolong Chief and Patriot* (Cape Town: Struik, 1966).

Plaatje, S. T., *Native Life in South Africa* (London, P.S. King and Co., 1916; new edition, Johannesburg, Ravan Press, 1983).

—, *Mhudi: an Epic of Native Life a Hundred Years Ago* (Alice: Lovedale Press, 1930; new edition, with Introduction by T.J. Couzens, London: Heinemann Educational Books, 1978).

Ross, Edward J., *Diary of the Siege of Mafeking, October 1899 to May 1900*, edited by B.P. Willan (Cape Town: Van Riebeeck Society, 1980).

Schapera, I., *A Handbook of Tswana Law and Custom* (London: International Institute of African Languages and Culture, 1938).

141

—, 'The System of Land Tenure on the Barolong Farms' (unpublished report to the Bechuanaland Protectorate Government, 1943).

—, *The Tswana* (London: Sidney Press, for the International African Institute Ethnographic Survey of Africa, 1953).

Sillery, A., *The Bechuanaland Protectorate* (Cape Town: Oxford University Press, 1952).

Stanislaus, Mother M., 'Diary of the Siege of Mafeking' (unpublished MS, Mafeking Museum).

Willan, B.P., *Sol Plaatje: South African Nationalist, 1876–1932* (London: Heinemann Educational Books, 1984; Berkeley, California: University of California Press, 1984; Johannesburg: Ravan Press, 1984).

Young, F., *The Relief of Mafeking* (London: Methuen, 1900).

Notes and References

INTRODUCTION

1 Letter to the Johannesburg *Star*, 5 July 1932.
2 *Plaatje* is not an indigenous name. According to family tradition, it was given to Plaatje's grandfather, Mogodi, by Dutch-speaking Griqua landownerrs when they lived in the Philippolis district. The word *plaatje* means 'flat' in Dutch, and was reputedly given to Mogodi because he had a flat-looking head.
3 For the early history and ethnology of the Barolong, see Breutz, *Tribes of the Mafeking District*. Today there are several Barolong chiefdoms. The four main branches of the former nation are named after their eponymous founders: Barolong boo Ratlou, Barolong boo Ratshidi, Barolong boo Rapulana and Barolong boo Seleka. The two that feature prominently in the text are the second and third; they were allied with Britain and the Boers respectively. In the notes they are referred to by the accepted foreshortenings, Tshidi-Barolong and Rapulana-Barolong (or simply, Tshidi and Rapulana). The fragmentation of the nation occurred c. 1780.
4 Cape Archives, Attorney-General (AG) 923, 189/1901 (Annexure B).
5 Plaatje, *Native Life in South Africa*, p. 17.
6 London *Times*, obituary notice (28 July 1932).
7 H. I. E. Dlhomo, 'An Appreciation' (*Umteteli wa Bantu*, 25 June 1932).

PROLOGUE

1 This represents a highly simplified and foreshortened background to a long and complex historical process. For a more complete picture, see Molema, *The Bantu Past and Present*, 1921, and *Montshiwa*, 1966; Agar-Hamilton, *The Road to the North*, 1937; Mackenzie, *Austral Africa*, 1887; Matthews, 'A Short History of the Tshidi-Barolong'.
2 Matthews, 'A Short History of the Tshidi-Barolong', p. 20.
3 *Loc. cit.*
4 Henceforth the European settlement is referred to as *Mafeking* and its Tshidi counterpart as *Mafikeng*.
5 Annexation occurred in 1896, ten years after Britain established British Bechuanaland. (See Sillery, *The Bechuanaland Protectorate*, 1952.)
6 Plaatje, *Native Life in South Africa*, pp. 239–40.
7 Although by the end of the siege almost 500 Barolong had actually taken up arms, the role of the 'natives' was, as the diary indicates, a point of contention throughout.

CHAPTER 1

OCTOBER–NOVEMBER 1899

1 Originally a Nguni term meaning (literally) 'not there'; now a popular South African colloquialism, it simply means 'no' when used thus. Its use in this context is interesting. Barolong, when speaking today of a violent man, often describe him as being Zulu; in the traditional world-view, the Zulu are associated with military strength – a notion that derives from perceived historical experience. Plaatje's use of a word that is commonly thought of in South Africa as being of Zulu origin, and its juxtaposition with 'terror', is obviously meant to be ironic. This is a day of peace – in a white man's war. The thunder referred to immediately before is probably used here to mean shelling or artillery bombardment, though Barolong speaking English sometimes use 'thunder' metaphorically to mean 'death'.

2 On 25 October, General Cronje (then head of the Boer forces) launched a heavy attack. The 94-pounder Creusot siege-gun – one of four bought from France – was set to work for the first time in earnest and was, with the rest of the Boer artillery, intended to pave the way for a two-pronged attack. Estimates of the number of attacks vary between 500 and 1 000. The force, however, was repelled. Altogether some 300 shells fell within the lines of investment.

3 The arrival of a relief-force was a constant subject of discussion. Any hopes at that time, however, must have been very remote as Colonel Plumer's regiment had been placed at Tuli near the Rhodesian border. Owing to the size and distance of his force, Plumer was in no position to attempt an attack on the besiegers. The arrival of troops from England had also been delayed.

4 Kanya (now officially spelt 'Kanye') is the capital of the Bangwaketse chiefdom. It lies approximately sixty miles north-north-west of Mafeking, in what is now Botswana.

5 Plaatje was a keen music-lover and musician. In the diary this is reflected in his predilection for the use of musical metaphor.

6 The 'Staats Artillerie' were responsible for the operation of Boer artillery. According to Grinnell-Milne (*Baden-Powell at Mafeking*, 1957, p. 106), many of these gunners were Germans lent from the Kaiser's army.

7 The Molopo flows through the stadt. Plaatje resided in a homestead near the river bank.

8 David Phooko, a distant relative of Plaatje's. Of Sotho origin, he was employed as a constable attached to the staff of the Inspector of Native Reserves at Mafeking from August 1899 to May 1900, and seems to have shared lodgings with Plaatje in the stadt. One survivor of the siege who knew Plaatje has proffered the information that David was the diarist's 'cousin' (the exact genealogical relationship is unclear as Tshidi use this term to denote a variety of classificatory relationships), as well as his closest friend.

9 The Payne family were a popular musical group from Australia, consisting of vocalists, violinists, pianists, flautists and bell-ringers. Plaatje would probably have seen them in March 1895 or January 1897, when they gave a number of performances in Kimberley.

10 The Jubilee Singers were a black American choir, popular with black and white audiences alike, who toured southern Africa on several occasions during the 1890s. Plaatje's recollections of them probably date from their visit to Kimberley in July 1895 and May 1896.

11 *Makasono* is the Tswana rendering of 'Maxim'. *Kgalema* literally translated means 'chide', 'scold', 'speak angrily' (J. Tom Brown, *Secwana–English Dictionary*, 1931). The use of the vernacular here is not arbitrary. It reflects a common

Barolong linguistic practice. When speaking English, Tswana words which have – for the speaker – either an onomatopoeic quality or greater descriptive suitability are used. *Makasono* has a staccato quality that is missing from its less descriptive English equivalent, and the *kg-* (*kga-lema*) represents a hard sound (ejective velar fricative) which is appropriate when used to indicate the implied emotion.

12 This is often used by Plaatje as shorthand to denote the Transvaal and Orange Free State republics.

13 Philemon Mahlelebe Moshoeshoe, warder at the Mafeking gaol. Formerly with the Basotho Mounted Police, he settled in Mafeking in 1894 and served as the local turnkey until 1912. During his early years there he was known as Philemon Mahlelebe, but after the siege reverted to his original family name, Moshoeshoe. Of Sotho origin, he became a naturalized member of the chiefdom in 1910. Plaatje refers to him as Philemon Mahlelebe.

14 Barnabas Samson was a well-known teacher, sometimes cited (erroneously) as the first African teacher in Mafeking. The Barolong predilection for nick-naming explains why he is referred to as 'Teacher' rather than by his first name. Like Philemon Moshoeshoe, Samson was of Sotho origin, and became a naturalized member of the chiefdom in 1910.

15 This is used to denote an African township or village. The term subsequently became synonymous with African urban concentrations throughout South Africa. Here it refers to what was originally the Fingo village (see below).

16 These Fingoes came from a tribe which lives on the south-eastern plain of southern Africa. They had been recruited to travel north with Rhodes' Pioneer Column nine years earlier. However, on arriving at Mafeking, they chose to remain and establish a village outside the stadt. During the siege this settlement was known as the Fingo location. There was also an urban location outside Mafeking. This was populated by Africans of mixed ethnic origin (as opposed to the Barolong village which was almost exclusively Tswana). This location existed until 1967, when its population was moved into the newly constructed Montshiwa Township. Unless otherwise specified, 'location' (in both text and notes) refers to the urban strangers' location and not the Fingo village.

17 These lay a mile out of the town as it was then constituted. As they were situated in the area of the line of investment, the territory was disputed throughout the siege. It subsequently became the scene of several skirmishes.

18 The population of the stadt used the river for purposes of sanitation in those days.

19 This ultimatum is not referred to in other siege records. Nor is it clear which were the prior ultimata. Perhaps he is alluding to the letter sent by General Cronje to Colonel Baden-Powell on the evening of 20 October in which the former gave a forty-eight hour warning of his intention to bombard the town, and added: 'You have to see that noncombatants leave Mafeking before the expiration of that time. If you do not comply with this I will not be answerable for the results.'

20 The Creusot siege-gun.

21 This village, also known as Rietfontein, was occupied by the Barolong boo Rapulana, who allied themselves with the Boers. Properly spelt Lotlhakane, it is approximately twelve miles south of Mafeking.

22 Such troop movements were common during this period of the siege, for Cronje hoped to open a path into the town through heavy artillery bombardment, followed by mounted attacks on weak points in the ring of defensive forts. That this was known to the besieged seems to indicate that at this time it was fairly easy to break the lines for intelligence purposes.

23 This is one of several names given to the Creusot siege-gun. The Boers termed

it 'Grietje'. The British, who found this difficult to pronounce, called it 'Creechy' which later developed into 'Creaky'. 'Big Ben' and 'Au Sanna' were two appellations the source of which is not clear. Plaatje uses 'Au Sanna' most frequently, although on occasion he does refer to the siege-gun as 'Big Ben'.

24 Makane was apparently the Serolong name for the Cannon Kopje area (see map). It is no longer used.

25 Dutch: 'pedestrian', 'hopper', 'wingless locust', 'infantry'. Plaatje, again using the most evocative term available – and obviously intending irony by referring deprecatingly to the Boers in their own language – probably had the last meaning in mind.

26 This gives the impression that the Boers and Barolong were constantly at war, which is perhaps an overstatement. They spent much time in verbal debate and mutual cattle-raiding but only fought in 1853 at Lotlhakane (after which Montshiwa and most of his followers fled to Moshaneng, near Kanye; the remainder, under Molema, founded Mafeking), again in 1881 (Sehuba) and in 1882 (Mafeking).

27 This refers to the war of 1881 in which the Rapulana-Barolong, dissatisfied by Montshiwa's attempts to exert jurisdiction over them, recruited the help of the Barolong boo Ratlou and a group of burghers, and forced the chief to remove from Sehuba to Mafeking (a distance of nine miles). It was as a result of this that Molema's village became the Tshidi-Barolong capital, and that land was given by the successful chiefs to the burghers to found the Republic of Goshen (at Rooigrond, eleven miles away). After Montshiwa fled to Mafikeng he *did* successfully resist attacks on the town (mounted by the same allies) during 1882.

28 Everyone was acutely aware that the battle was crucial to the fate of Mafeking. Baden-Powell deployed supportive artillery which played a major part in the successful defence. Plaatje is probably trying to say that nobody cared to go to their assistance because of the strategic danger involved.

29 Estimates of the number of defenders in the Cannon Kopje (Makane) fort vary widely, and no two sources agree. Plaatje's estimate of seventy is the highest. In his diary, J. Angus Hamilton (*Siege of Mafeking*, 1900, p. 99) states that the defence was 'a mere gun emplacement and forty-four men . . .' Major F. D. Baillie's diary (*Mafeking*, p. 40) claims that the force was 'fifty-seven strong', while Grinnell-Milne (*Baden-Powell at Mafeking*, p. 91) puts the number at fifty.

30 Common among all parties was the strategy of 'playing dead' until the cover of night made escape possible. This ruse is frequently mentioned both in written records and was recalled by survivors. Apparently there existed a widespread dread of capture as stories about the treatment of prisoners on both sides emphasized a horror of this fate.

31 This spelling, like that for much of the vernacular in the text, is a function of the orthographic confusion of the era. *Thota*-ing (Sotho) or *Thutha*-ing (Xhosa-Zulu) is intended. It means 'carry' or 'transport'. The English suffix -*ing* is clearly meant as a joke. Humour through wordplay is a characteristic of the text, as it is of the author's cultural background.

32 Here again figures vary. That two officers (Captains Marsham and Pechell) were killed is, however, certain.

33 Plaatje's esteem for Captain Marsham was shared both by the garrison and by the beleaguered citizenry. Major Baillie (*Mafeking*, 1900, p. 40) predicted that, even among the enemy, regret over his death would be widespread, for his popularity was not limited by the line of investment. Much was made of the gallantry of his death, for it is reported that he died while assisting a wounded comrade.

34 The importance of this battle has, perhaps, been underplayed by the diarist.

The military strategists among the defenders were quite aware that Cannon Kopje was at one and the same time a vital and a weak link in the defences. Being the highest point in the area it had clear vantage over the town, and all were adamant that, had it fallen, Mafeking would have become indefensible. That Cannon Kopje was a weak link in the defences is explained by the fact that, in order to render it impregnable, it would have been necessary to blast away some of the rock of which the hill is entirely constituted. The rush to prepare the town's more immediate defence needs, it is argued, made it impossible to attend to this post before the siege was laid. Furthermore, dynamite was at the time a scarce commodity, for with it Baden-Powell created an important ruse: he ordered the burying of boxes in the ground along the perimeter and spread the word (the spies in Mafeking being particularly useful in this regard) that a mine-field had been planted. This might explain, to some extent, why Cannon Kopje was under-fortified.

35 This refers to the Cannon Kopje battle. Murchison commanded the artillery that supported the defenders from the south of the Molopo, attacking the Boer flank with seven-pounder shells.

36 Parslow was the war correspondent of the *Daily Chronicle*. He was also to have assisted Whales, the editor of the *Mafeking Mail*, whose first siege-edition came out on this day. (It was subsequently issued daily, 'shells permitting'.) For reasons much speculated upon but never disclosed, Murchison shot the journalist through the head. He was later condemned to death by a court martial, but this sentence was commuted to life penal servitude by Lord Roberts on the advice of Baden-Powell.

37 In the capacity of interpreter and typist.

38 It must be remembered that the siege took place during the rainy season. Barolong, who depended largely on the elements for the success of their agricultural and pastoral activities, tended to worry obsessively about the weather. In this Plaatje is no exception – as later entries will prove.

39 The Kgalagadi were once thought of by ethnologists as impoverished Batswana who had taken to the desert when the other Tswana tribes migrated into eastern Botswana. While the latter is true, it has come to light that they are a separate division of the Sotho-speaking group of peoples. Traditionally some of their number formed (along with the Sarwa bushmen) a class of serfs among the stronger Tswana tribes. Today, however, they are simply commoners in these tribes. (See Schapera, *The Tswana*, 1953; Kuper, *Kalahari Village Politics*, 1970).

40 The women's laager (Dutch: 'encampment') was set up some distance from the town itself in order to concentrate the beleaguered women and children at a site safe from shelling. As no one envisaged that the siege would be lengthy, the encampment always remained temporary in its structure. Although most women sought safety in the laager, some preferred to remain in town. The encampment was set up on the instruction of Colonel Baden-Powell.

41 *Laar* in this context is an abbreviated form of the word *laager*.

42 The Creusot siege-gun was often fired in the evening at about nine o'clock. As this invariably was only one round it became known by the besieged populace as the 'good-night' shot. Plaatje, who obviously saw the irony in this, altered the appellation and throughout the diary refers to it as the gun's 'bad-night'.

43 The strategy of using the railway line to propel explosives at the enemy had been used before. At the beginning of the siege (13 October) the armoured train was loaded with dynamite, and two trucks allowed to run down an incline towards Boers who weere engaged in pulling up the rails to the north of the town.

44 Jackal Tree was, throughout the siege, the most common position for the Creusot siege-gun. Although this 94-pounder was moved on several occasions,

Jackal Tree was most advantageous as it put Cannon Kopje and the town within close range.

45 'Barolongs' is an erroneous usage, being a double plural. The Setswana class-two subjectival concord *ba*- itself represents the plural. This usage is, still today, common among Barolong. In fact, its origin dates back to early European contact, when the grammatical structure of the language had not been documented. Folk linguists claim that Barolong use began through the mimicking of Europeans.

46 'Paul' is Paul Marumolwa, also known as Paul Montshiwa. He was a cousin (father's brother's son) to the chief of the Tshidi-Barolong, Wessels Montshiwa. The Tshidi had a system of named age-regiments to which young men were recruited. One of the traditional functions of these was the waging of war. Each regiment had a leader who was a son or close agnatic kinsman of the chief. In the case of this regiment the leader was Paul.

47 Harland Bell, a corporal in the Bechuanaland Rifles, and son of Charles Bell, Magistrate and Civil Commissioner.

48 Baden-Powell's letter to Cronje warned of 'regrettable retribution' if the Boers persisted in shelling the women's laager, the hospital and the convent. Cronje replied that he had fired upon the convent because the British had mounted guns in that building. Although the *Mafeking Mail* (9 November) denies that this was so, Mother Mary Stanislaus writes in her unpublished diary that there was, in fact, an artillery emplacement in the convent. Later this was explained by apologists on the British side by the fact that the Boers had persisted in shelling the building, despite warnings, and that therefore Baden-Powell was simply paying them back in kind. Throughout the siege this was a bone of contention, and a considerable amount of correspondence passed between the respective commanders over it.

49 The passage in parentheses is written in the margin and is incomplete.

50 This entry is written against the two dates and is undifferentiated.

51 Weil's Store made an important contribution to the survival of the besieged population. Ben Weil had, with amazing foresight, laid in tremendous stocks of foodstuffs and other necessities before the siege. With the other local merchants he played a major role in solving Baden-Powell's greatest problem; their supplies, together with a railway consignment which had been held up in Mafeking before investment, provided an important source of food.

52 All efforts to find information on these two people have failed. Barolong despatch-runners were very useful to the British garrison for, knowing the country intimately, they managed often to slip through the Boer lines and return with news both of the outside world and of enemy troop movements.

53 Situated approximately eighteen miles north-west of Mafeking, this village was occupied by Barolong of the same tribe as those in the besieged town.

54 Ga-molimola (or Modimola) is also a Barolong boo Ratshidi village. It is thirteen miles due west of Mafeking.

55 i.e., the headman.

56 This paragraph is lightly crossed out in the original text. The incident to which the diarist refers is the arrival of the Warren Expedition in the district in early 1885. For several years before there had been land disputes between Boer and Barolong (see notes 23 and 24 above). Cecil Rhodes, then British Deputy Commissioner in Bechuanaland, advised the British Government to send a strong force 'to restore order in Bechuanaland and to defend the Native tribes who had placed themselves under British protection'. (Matthews, 'Short History of the Tshidi-Barolong', 1945, p. 20.) The Warren Expedition dispersed the citizens of the Goshen Republic but there is no reference to reparations or return of cattle in the available literature. Plaatje thus raises an interesting

historical point. (For full accounts of this incident, see Matthews, 'Short History of the Tshidi-Barolong', 1945; Molema, *Montshiwa*, 1966.)

57 Stephen Lefenya, who held the position of secretary to Chief Montshiwa and his successors, was an important personality in tribal affairs. He later became a chiefly emissary and often negotiated with both British and Boers on matters affecting the tribe.

58 These are 'farms' owned by the Barolong in what was then the Bechuanaland Protectorate. (See Schapera, 'The System of Land Tenure on the Barolong Farms,' 1943.)

59 The entire entry is lightly deleted, for no apparent reason. The insertion in parentheses is written in pencil at the top of the relevant page. Already a habitual manipulator of language for the sake of humour, he appears to be experimenting with alliteration here.

60 This was the home of the Resident Commissioner, Mr C. G. H. Bell.

61 This was the Tswana name given by the Barolong to General Cronje. The prefix *ra* (properly *rra*) here means 'father', though it may be used, very broadly, in relation to any adult male. *Ntho'akgale* (Sotho-Tswana) is a combinative term – *ntho* being a 'bruise', 'sore' or 'leprosy', and *akgale* meaning 'of the past'. Thus the nickname personified by the prefix *rra* may be translated as 'an old sore'. Its derogatory nature reflects the fact that the Barolong saw the Boer commander as a long-time enemy.

62 A small African child. This word – derived from Portuguese – has become a South African colloquialism. Its use here gives us an insight into Plaatje's study of literary style. On Monday, the thirteenth, we saw how he experimented with alliteration. 'The pate of a piccaninny' is a contrived phrase which the author introduces – almost self-consciously, it seems – in order to give expression to a newly acquired literary technique. As elsewhere, we see here the function of the diary as an exercise in the study of literary skills, and watch Plaatje, the scholar, maturing.

63 A small village with grazing-lands, some two miles to the west of the stadt.

64 The war correspondents in Mafeking were G. N. Whales (Cape Press), who also edited the *Mafeking Mail*, Vere Stent (Reuters), J. E. Neilly (*Pall Mall Gazette*), J. Angus Hamilton (the London *Times*) and F. D. Baillie (the *Morning Post*). Plaatje's services, as typist and interpreter, were in demand among these men for whom secretarial help must have been in short supply.

65 Mr E. G. Parslow, the deceased correspondent of the *Daily Chronicle*.

66 The alarm system worked as follows: whenever sentries observed the gunners elevating the barrel of 'Big Ben' someone was sent off to ring the alarm bells. This gave the townspeople a few minutes to take cover. The Boers, however, learnt of this, and after readying the gun, left it for a while. As a result the warning-system became less reliable.

67 The 94-pounder.

68 General Cronje actually left on the eighteenth. According to Grinnell-Milne (*Baden-Powell at Mafeking*, 1957, p. 109) he took 6 000 men with him, leaving the succeeding commander, Snyman, with 4 000. The departure of Cronje signalled the beginning of a new strategy on the part of the Boers.

69 There is no report of this elsewhere, and either the diarist is the only one to record the incident, or he was misled by the fact that the gun was moved to a new position on the seventeenth.

70 The 'American' was J. E. Pearson, a correspondent for Reuters, who had travelled from Cape Town. He made his way through Boer lines into Mafeking on 11 November.

71 All figures show evidence of multiple alteration in the text.

72 This sentence is phrased clumsily in the text. The editor has taken the liberty of rewording it in order to render it comprehensible.

73 St Leger ('Sainty'), named after F. Y. St Leger, a well-known newspaper editor, was Plaatje's son, now one year old. St Leger had left Mafeking with his mother in August 1899 to visit her family in Burghersdorp, and they did not return to Mafeking until after the siege.

74 Probably Silas Molema, a descendant of the founder of Mafeking. One of the Tshidi–Barolong nobility, he had recommended Plaatje to Charles Bell when he had applied for his job as court interpreter in 1898, and subsequently financed *Koranta ea Becoana* ('The Bechuana Gazette'), the newspaper which Plaatje edited after the siege.

75 He appeared before the court again the next day and, owing to lack of evidence, was convicted of improper, rather than treasonable, conduct (*Mafeking Mail*, 25 November).

76 When the siege began Baden-Powell declared martial law in the town. There seemed to be no clear division of functions between its different courts. It was not simply a matter of courts martial dealing with judicial matters among the militia and the Court of Summary Jurisdiction handling civilian misdemeanours. The latter often sat before military men (especially Major Goold-Adams, Colonel C. B. Vyvyan and Major Lord Edward Cecil) while the Preliminary Examination in the Parslow murder case was heard by the Resident Magistrate, C. G. H. Bell. Only later was that trial transferred to a Field General Court Martial. Roughly speaking, however, the division of labour did fall along the lines of the military or civilian status of the accused. Plaatje worked for the Court of Summary Jurisdiction as a (Dutch-English-Setswana) translator and later as a shorthand secretary.

77 Entries from the 24th to the 26th are written in a completely different handwriting. The second style appears again later on in the diary. Plaatje offers no explanation for it, but as these passages are notable for the frequency of spelling errors and lack of punctuation it is possible that he dictated them to someone who wrote them for him. The style and content, however, are unmistakably Plaatje's.

78 'Close-up' probably means parting or final (in this case, shot).

79 The actual entry in Bell's diary (for 26 November) reads: 'The Boers come out of their trenches and sit in long rows on the embankment and gaze upon Mafeking with covetous eyes; and they [Bell later deleted 'they'] no doubt marvel at our holding out so long, after five weeks of continuous shelling. They cannot understand what has become of us as they never see any one: and the rat-tat of the Maxim and the pop of the Lee Metford are the only sounds emanating from this mysterious town.'

80 In fact this paragraph is also a close paraphrase, only slightly changed, of Bell's diary entry.

81 By 'cut down below' Plaatje almost certainly meant 'cut off down below'. 'Bud' refers to Isaiah Bud-M'belle, brother-in-law and close friend of Plaatje's, who was based in Kimberley as interpreter in 'native languages' in the Griqualand West High Court, Special and Circuit Courts. He had been cut off from Kimberley at the start of the war while on circuit duty with the Judge President in the north-eastern Cape.

CHAPTER 2

DECEMBER 1899

1 Kuruman, the site of much of Robert Moffat's mission work among the Batlharo, is approximately 190 miles from Mafeking. It lies in a south-westerly direction.

2 The *Vierkleur* (Dutch: literally, 'four colour') was the flag of the Transvaal Republic. It had a vertical green stripe, and horizontal orange, white and blue stripes.

3 This is a Barolong boo Ratlou village in the Vryburg district.

4 Letlhogile was chief of the Mariba branch of the Barolong boo Ratlou tribe of Ganyesa. The Ratlou are not to be confused with the Barolong boo Rapulana who allied themselves with the Boers.

5 The actual word written in the text is indecipherable and the editor has taken the liberty of introducing 'Au Sanna', as this was clearly the diarist's intended meaning.

6 The relevant report in the *Mafeking Mail* of 1 December reads as follows: 'The Boers had two pieces of artillery knocked out by us at the Waterworks affair on October 23rd.' The battle alluded to was one fought solely between the artillerists, and there had been considerable speculation as to its real outcome before this report arrived.

7 This is an understatement of the size of the garrison (see Prologue, p. 18).

8 Dutch: 'patch of ground'. Again Plaatje chooses to use a Dutch word, and again it does not appear to be an arbitrary choice. The area concerned was interstitial and dangerous; to stray into it was to move into the realm of Boer control. The diarist's use of Dutch reflects this – the correlation between the introduction of another language and its sociological reference is too frequent to be arbitrary.

9 Mr F. Whiteley was the Mayor of Mafeking before and during the siege.

10 Many such false reports arrived in Mafeking. Kimberley was only relieved on 15 February, and the first reliable report reached Mafeking in the last weeek of that month.

11 Tswana: 'greet', 'salute'.

12 Linchwe (or Lentswe) was chief of the Bakgatla tribe at Mochudi in the Bechuanaland Protectorate. Before the war he sent his brother, Segale, to negotiate with the Boers on the basis that although this was a white man's war, he would resist any attempt to violate his territory. At the same time he promised not to act as aggressor (which he could not have done anyway as he lacked the strength). The Boers, for reasons which have often been hotly debated, overran two Bakgatla villages without facing resistance. Soon after Lentswe's warriors ambushed an ammunition convoy in the Marico district. With the conquered arms they repulsed what were alleged to be two further invasions (the exact location of these confrontations being unclear), and entered Boer territory. It is to this expedition that Plaatje's entry refers.

13 Kgamaco was a daughter of Chief Wessels Montshiwa by his first wife, Keleco (Keletso) Saane Tawana.

14 Senobe Saane Tawana, the youngest of Wessels Montshiwa's wives. Senobe, like Keleco, was a daughter of Chief Saane of Modimola.

15 This usage represents a linguistic mixture: *-azi* or *-kazi* are Nguni feminine suffixes; the *k* (of Nguni) is pronounced as *h* when transposed into Sotho-Tswana (*k→h* is a regular sound-shift). Hence the word means 'Barolong women'.

16 This is Sotho-Tswana. Exact translation is difficult as the word *fela* (or *hela*) has more than one meaning. In Sotho it is an auxiliary verb that means 'certainly' or 'indeed'. In Tswana it can mean 'everything', 'all' or 'certainly'; as an auxiliary verb it means 'to continue'. Thus in Sotho the sentence may be translated as 'They might indeed (certainly) have killed them'. In Tswana the most appropriate translation would seem to be 'They might have killed them all'.

17 The officer referred to was Gordon Wilson. His wife, Lady Sarah (daughter of the Duke of Marlborough), took refuge at Setlagoli (some fifty miles south-west of Mafeking) at the beginning of the siege. The place, Mosita, referred to

in the same sentence, is approximately twenty miles west of Setlagoli and 55 miles south-west of Mafeking.

18 *Redan:* 'A fortification with two parapets meeting at a salient angle'.

19 These were the Irish Sisters of Mercy who occupied the convent; they were removed to safer accommodation when shelling in their vicinity became heavy.

20 *Mafeking Mail*, 6 December. Plaatje has reproduced the article in full.

21 *Go thiba* (Tswana): 'to turn back', 'stop', 'obstruct', etc. The actual word in the text is difficult to decipher, but this seems most possible and comprehensible. The word is also used in Sotho, but its meaning ('stop', 'obstruct', 'prevent', 'impede', etc.) is slightly different. The Sotho-Tswana range of meaning is most apt to describe the operation. Again here Plaatje chooses a Tswana word to describe a sphere of action that, during the siege, belonged to the Africans alone.

22 Possibly Matshane Meko. Nothing more of him is known beyond the fact that he took part in the defence.

23 The Reuters war-correspondent.

24 This is a Tswana verb. It means 'to lie down to be beaten' or 'beaten when lying down'. The English suffix *-ing* transposes the sense of the word from verb to gerund. Plaatje's use of the vernacular in an unexpected context (and its juxtaposition with the English suffix *-ing*) succeeds in conveying the humour in a tragic situation.

25 Orpheus M. McAdoo was the proprietor and director of the Jubilee Singers. After this group split up, he continued to perform with a number of its original members, and they were known either as 'McAdoo's Minstrels' or 'McAdoo's Vaudevilles'. They visited Kimberley in April 1898.

26 Probably a translation of the Dutch *baster*: 'person of mixed ethnic stock'.

27 Xhosa-Zulu: 'leopard'. Southern Bantu frequently use animal allegory. Here the leopard, as an animal of prey, is a metaphor for the greatest threat to the besieged town – the Creusot siege-gun.

28 This is the phonetic spelling of Viljoen. Lady Sarah's arrival was treated as something of a festive occasion, and her romantic escapades became a talking-point for the news-hungry townspeople.

29 Dutch: 'angry' or 'hot-tempered'.

30 This word definitely appears in the text. It is not clear what meaning is intended.

31 Properly *isinge* (Xhosa). A class 7 noun, it means 'back'.

32 In fact Plaatje omits it completely. However, as it was printed in the *Mafeking Mail* of 11 December, it is reproduced here in full.

33 It is reported that Baden-Powell refused at first to consent to the exchange, but that Lord Edward Cecil persuaded him to accept the Boer demand.

34 Plaatje often uses the word 'herd' instead of 'shepherd' or 'herdsman' in the text.

35 Presumably a near-by Boer laager.

36 Dutch: 'straps' or 'thongs'.

37 At the time of the siege Bokone was about a mile from the centre of the stadt. In its subsequent growth the village eventually encompassed this area. *Bokone* (Setswana) means 'north'.

38 Xhosa: 'scarce'. By using a non-Tswana word, Plaatje emphasizes how prized this loot must have been to the envious non-Tswana men of the 'Black Watch'.

39 When Barolong speak in English, of judicial proceedings, they tend to say 'the case is . . . (for example, adultery)'. This results from the direct translation of Setswana usage. Hence we may guess that Plaatje is trying to say that the case arising out of this incident was one of 'sticking up' (i.e., robbery).

40 Cornelius Gaboutloeloe, a local headman and Wesleyan lay-preacher. He was in charge of the Barolong cattle guard during the siege.
41 Or *Qhuma*. Zulu: 'pop', 'crack' or 'burst'. The click pronunciation of the *q*, suggests onomatopoeia.
42 Used synonymously with 'Kgalagari'. Some Sotho-Tswana consonants are used interchangeably. This also explains 'Bakgalagalis' in the next sentence but one. Both 'Kalahari' and 'Bakgalagali' are frequently used by contemporary Barolong.
43 Dutch: 'five hundred' and 'ten hundred' respectively. The Dutch is probably used here to emphasize the authenticity of the report – it implies an admission by the Boers. It may also be that 'tien honderd' is preferred to 'a thousand' in order to emphasize that Boer losses were double those of the English.
44 Here he uses the original Barolong name for Mafeking. It is the locative form of the word *mafika* ('rocks').
45 Tau was the last effective ruler of a united Barolong people. He died in about 1760, and it was in the lifetime of his sons that the Barolong divided into four branches. The name Tau means 'Lion'. In fact, the Barolong migrated southwards before 1750, and there is no record of their having lived in Ngamiland. Furthermore, *Mafikeng* was founded – and named – approximately a century after the death of Tau. But this is not simply erroneous history; it reflects one important aspect of the Tshidi-Barolong conscious model of their relations with the Boers.
46 Tswana: literally, 'they who are uplifted and fierce'. The expression, according to one Tshidi informant, implies that they were supernaturally inspired. One point of clarification: the second word of the sentence (*rungwana:* 'lifted up', 'raised', 'uplifted') has a diminutive suffix. This can, and may here, be used to convey affection.
47 A British newspaper for which Angus Hamilton wrote frequently during the siege.
48 Reverend Briscoe was the Methodist missionary in the stadt. The mission-house stands opposite the 'Warren' church (built in 1855 by Warren's engineers) across the Molopo. The drift was the point at which the river could be crossed between the church and the mission-house, and was close to Plaatje's home.
49 A species of tree common in the district.
50 i.e., Cornelius Gaboutloeloe (see note 37).
51 Tiego was the son of Selere, the younger brother of the late chief Montshiwa. He was a cousin (father's brother's son) of Wessels, the chief during the siege, and later became a prominent man in tribal politics. The 'corps' referred to is the age-regiment of which Tiego was leader. Having been formed in 1892, it was the most recently founded at the time.
52 i.e., the railway line.
53 Plaatje probably did not bother to copy out the proclamation as it was printed both as a hand-out and an article in the *Mafeking Mail*. From his mention of the 'accompanying circular', we may guess that the diarist slipped a copy into his notebook, and that this was lost. It is therefore reproduced here in full.
54 The Zuid-Afrikaansche Republiek, established after the first Anglo-Boer War (1880). Paul Kruger became its president in 1883.
55 This despatch also carried an angry retort from Snyman. The *Mafeking Mail* (13 December) reports the communication as follows: 'General Snyman has written with regard to Colonel Baden-Powell's circular addressed to the Burghers. He is very incensed at its having been sent direct to them, and is apparently much annoyed at the remark that "sitting down and looking at a

place is not the way to take it". He challenges us to come out and drive them
away. He also explains that, far from the Burghers being kept in the dark by
their commanders and newspapers, the opposite is the case . . .'

56 Lord Methuen, a former Governor of Natal, was appointed Commander of
the First Division Army Corps when the war broke out. A successful soldier
in many African campaigns, he was heavily defeated at Magersfontein on
11 December. The news that the British army had lost over 1 000 men in this
battle had not yet reached Mafeking.

57 'Sibale' refers to Patrick Sidzumo, messenger of the magistrate's court
in Mafeking, while 'uninikazi' refers to his wife, Martha Sidzumo (née
Mvungama). Both 'Sibale' (Xhosa: *sibali*, a brother-in-law) and 'uninikazi'
(Xhosa: *uninakazi*, his maternal aunt) are used to specify the relationship
between the diarist and the Sidzumos. Plaatje was related to the Sidzumos
through marriage, his wife Elizabeth (née M'belle) being related to Patrick's
mother, Sarah Sidzumo (née Mabandla. Both the M'belles and Sidzumos
were of Mfengu origin, thus Plaatje's choice of Xhosa terms.

58 i.e., back from the stadt to the house in the location.

59 Plaatje implies here that most of their news was secured by Barolong spies.

60 *Mafeking Mail*, 18 December. Probably Plaatje had fallen behind with his
entries and brought them up to date subsequently – which would explain the
use of an extract from the *Mail* from a date later than his diary entry.

61 The last three paragraphs show evidence of multiple alteration. The editor
has taken the liberty of reproducing the most coherent version possible. The
'old general' was obviously Joubert.

62 'The liar' mentioned by Plaatje is the 'notorious liar' of whom Bell writes, and
his 'interesting item' relates to the claims made about the big gun's removal.
Bell wrote of the man: 'His crime was "not speaking the truth" . . . He went
one evening, to the Boer lines to steal, and returned next day stating that the
big gun had been removed, during the night. As this was found to be untrue,
and as the culprit was a notorious liar, and having no friends here, it was
thought as well to shoot him as an example to others.' (Bell, 'Diary', 25 December,
p. 76).

63 *Hamba* (Xhosa) and *inkomo* (Zulu) mean 'go' and 'head of cattle' respectively.
The combination is intended to mean 'to move cattle' – i.e., to raid. It is a
clumsy usage; for the sake of exactitude, if nothing else, the verb should be
written as a causative (*hambisa*). Plaatje, who is usually fastidious in his
Bantu usage, may be using linguistic clumsiness to reflect the clumsiness of
the operation. While this interpretation may appear to flatter the diarist,
comparison with his use of language to reflect behaviour in other contexts
makes this explanation possible. The use of Zulu suggests that the men
concerned were non-Tswana living in the location. (Had they been members
of the Black Watch special mention would probably have been made.)

64 Barolong families who could command the necessary resources tended to
build European-style homesteads. These generally had a few outhouses built
in the manner of traditional huts.

65 Setuki Legalatladi Lekoma. The Lekomas were a large and influential Tshidi-
Barolong family group.

66 Celebrated on 16 December, this is the anniversary of the defeat of 10 000 of
Dingaan's Zulus by a party of Boer trekkers at the battle of Blood River in
Natal, in 1838.

67 The acting Chief Staff Officer at this time was Major Panzera, who also
commanded the artillery. The permanent C.S.O. was Lord Edward Cecil.

68 This should be written as one word (*walimala*). Being Xhosa-Zulu, it is in the
stative and means 'he was injured (hurt, crippled, etc.)'.

69 Dutch: 'out of shape'. In a footnote Plaatje adds that the bridle subsequently
broke.

70 This and half of the next entry and again written in the second handwriting
     alluded to above. The fact that Plaatje was at this time laid up with influenza
     adds weight to the opinion that these passages were dictated by him to an
     unknown scribe. Here, as in the previous case, spelling and punctuation
     degenerate, words are omitted and careless errors abound. Immediately on
     the resumption of Plaatje's own script, these shortcomings are eliminated.
     (See notes to the entry of 24 November above.)

71 Plaatje himself had moved to Mafeking in October 1898 to begin his new job
     in the office of the Resident Magistrate and Civil Commissioner, but Elizabeth
     did not join him there until early in 1899, several months after St Leger was
     born.

72 Mrs Diamond. There is no way of expressing 'Mrs' in Tswana. A married
     woman is referred to by the prefix *Mma* (literally 'mother'), followed by her
     husband's or son's name. 'Ma-Diamond' is probably Mrs Lesoane, mother of
     Diamond Lesoane.

73 Dutch: 'a small rag, or cloth'. It is probable that he intended some item of
     clothing.

74 Tswana: 'the thing (unspecified) that belongs to my elder brother'. *Bhuti*,
     translated here as 'elder brother', is not actually Tswana. It is a Nguni
     corruption of the Dutch *boetie* (brother) that is sometimes heard among
     Barolong. The phrase may be a euphemism for something of which direct
     mention is avoided.

75 The Christmas celebrations were indeed elaborate. Lady Sarah Wilson and
     Ben Weil organized a tea-party, complete with decorated tree, for some 250
     children of the town. Sports were arranged for the adults in the afternoon.
     Judging from the reports of lavish dinners, the atmosphere in town appears
     to have belied its besieged state. There are no reports of celebrations in the
     stadt, but it would seem that the Barolong had to rely on spiritual rather than
     culinary satisfaction.

76 Baden-Powell 'rescheduled' Christmas because of his belief that the Boers
     celebrate New Year rather than this holy day. In fact, there were no hostilities
     from either side on the 25th.

77 Plaatje and Elizabeth M'belle were married by civil licence in Kimberley on
     25 January 1898, in the face of opposition from both families, who dis-
     approved of them marrying outside their respective ethnic groups. This is
     probably what Plaatje is referring to when he describes the path to his
     'union' with Elizabeth as 'rocky'.

78 Or *mogodi*. Tswana: 'a leader', 'distinguished one'. Plaatje may have intended
     a pun here, for *godi* means 'gunpowder' (the *mo-* in this context being the
     class-one subjectival concord implying a person).

79 Several reasons have been advanced for Baden-Powell's decision to attack
     Game Tree, a Boer fort to the north-east of the town. Among them, the need
     for more pasturage, for a morale-booster, and for retaining some initiative
     are the three most quoted. But secondary reasons – the neutralization of the
     point from which the convent, hospital and the women's laager were being
     shelled and the opening of a way for a relief column – have also been
     suggested.
       The Boers got wind of the impending attack and strengthened their
     fortifications to good effect. Two squadrons of the Protectorate Regiment,
     under captains FitzClarence and Vernon (who was killed) advanced, with
     support from the armoured train and artillery. They met heavy fire and
     registered more losses than in any other confrontation. The final casualty-list
     included 24 killed, 23 wounded, and 3 captured. (Plaatje's figures are more
     accurate than any other siege-diarists' here.)

80 Stories about Lenkoane. Evidently 'Hyena Jones' was Lenkoane's nickname.
     Plaatje had known Patrick Lenkoane well in Kimberley. Of Sotho origin,

Lenkoane had once worked for Cecil Rhodes, later described himself as a boarding-house keeper, and was renowned in Kimberley's African community for his sense of humour and his comical behaviour.

81 Zulu-Xhosa: properly spelt *'lingana'*, it means 'to be equal to'. It has been suggested to me that the reference here is to time; the devil knows the exact measurement of his remaining time by measuring it against a tape.

82 i.e., 'better'.

83 'Mma, ke tseba . . . my wife is at work.' The four sentences are, with the exception of the Tswana auxiliary verb *mma* ('look here', 'wait a minute'), mainly a mixture of Southern Sotho and Hyena's Sotho-accented English. The first sentence means 'Look here, I know the enmity of people such as Phooko' (i.e., David Phooko, who related the story to Plaatje). The second sentence ('When are you going to adopt the ways of civilised people?') is a representation of Sotho-accented English. Its accuracy is, I am told, remarkable – especially in regard to the emphasis of consonants. The third sentence – with the exception of *chata* (Xhosa: 'marry') – is again Southern Sotho, and means 'I have just now (got) married.' The fourth sentence is clear, with only the *g-* (gentleman) being replaced by *ch-*.

The story of Hyena Jones, the comic, is a playful satire characterized by linguistic imitation. Plaatje recounts with obvious mirth Hyena's exaggerated claim to be dying, and his remarkable recovery brought about by David's questions. The bragging and the cowardice with which Hyena intended to settle the 'love question' is juxtaposed with his hurt ('On one occasion . . . at work') at the fact that people like David Phooko would gossip about his wife earning money for him. Hyena is the personification of a human foible: he moralizes about the undesirability of men being supported by their wives – and lies in order to deny that he is such a man.

84 The allusion here is to one of the books from which Plaatje learned English. It was published by Nelson's, and was widely used in schools throughout the English-speaking world. Plaatje is remembering a story called 'The Wonderful Pudding', in which an uncle asks two boys to dinner, promising them a pudding, 'the materials of which had given work to more than a thousand men'. Expecting to find an enormous pudding when they arrived, the two boys were surprised to 'find everything calm and quiet as usual', and then disappointed when a normal-sized plum-pudding is brought to the dinner table for them to eat. After they had eaten some of it, their uncle then explains how even a small pudding, in view of its many ingredients, requires the work of over a thousand people. (*Nelson's Royal Reader III*, London, 1872, pp. 26–8.)

85 Mr Bell, the Civil Commissioner.

86 Fourteen Streams is located on the Vaal River near the Cape–Transvaal border. Phokwane (Pokwani) lies in the vicinity of Hartswater, midway between Vryburg and Kimberley. (There is no settlement at Fourteen Streams. The nearest town is Warrenton.)

87 Belmont lies approximately 55 miles south of Kimberley.

88 President Kruger of the Transvaal.

89 Dutch: 'hillock'.

90 The latter half of the entry for 28 December and the first paragraph of that of the 28th are again written in the second handwriting. As explained above, the necessary corrections have been made.

91 The only bank in town at the time. When shelling became heavy, it was transferred to an underground shelter and operated from there.

92 Properly *amahlwempu* (sing. *ihlwempu*). Xhosa: 'the needy people'.

93 'Lekoko' is Lekoko Marumolwa, commonly known as Lekoko Montshiwa. He was a cousin (father's brother's son) to Chief Wessels. An older man of

considerable political influence among the Tshidi, Lekoko was the effective tribal leader during the siege. He assumed this position formally in January 1900 when Wessels was deposed by the military authorities because of his lack of co-operation and 'inability to duly perform his duties as Chief' (General Orders, 1 January). Wessels, however, was reinstated as tribal head after the siege.

94 In this instance 'he' refers to Baden-Powell.
95 This is an interesting aside on the attack which is not documented elsewhere. That Plaatje had access to it is quite possible, for he spent much time in the company of the most senior of Baden-Powell's staff. This remark is most relevant in assessing both the propriety of the decision to attack the fort, and the real reasons for it. (See notes for the entry of the 26th.) One obvious possibility that has not been considered is the eagerness of the garrison to 'have a go' at the Boers, and we know that pressure of this sort was brought to bear on Baden-Powell later on in the siege.
96 Baden-Powell; he took up his position at Fort Dummy, which lay between the town and Game Tree.
97 Probably Mr W. Cowen, originally from West Africa, whom Plaatje had known in Kimberley. It has not been possible to identify the particular case mentioned.
98 Alarm-bells.
99 The Maseloas were among the oldest-established families in Mafikeng, having settled there with Molema Tawana in 1857.
100 Jameson had been in Mafeking just prior to the siege, but left before hostilities began. Perhaps this reference to Jameson was jocular: he had been defeated easily before, why not again?
101 The case of theft in the women's laager, mentioned above.
102 Dutch: 'old-year's day'.
103 Thelesho was the fifth son of Molema, the founder of *Mafikeng* and a brother of Silas Molema. The family group of which he was a member frequently acted as a faction in opposition to the ruling descendants of Montshiwa and their political supporters. Thelesho was, until his death some years later, a very active tribal politician. The issue referred to concerned Chief Wessels' alleged mismanagement of Tshidi tribal affairs.
104 Joel Nyangi was an intelligence officer and office messenger attached to the Railway Division during the siege. He also saw active service with the Railway Contingent, being wounded on two occasions (14 October and 13 February).
105 It is not clear who is meant by 'he' in this case.
106 The use of 'former' and 'latter' here is confusing; both would seem to relate more appropriately to the grain issue than to any other mentioned.

CHAPTER 3

JANUARY 1900

1 Plaatje is questioning the applicability of the diminutive suffix *je* in the gun's nickname. Why should such a powerful weapon be referred to diminutively when 'Griet' (without the diminutive) would reflect her potency more aptly?
2 'Ebie' is Solomon Ebenezer Schiemann, Plaatje's cousin. His mother, Leah Schiemann, was a sister of Sol Plaatje's father, Johannes Kushumane Plaatje.

Ebie, who came from Pniel, was staying with Plaatje in Mafeking when the town was besieged. He celebrated his sixth birthday during the siege. ·

3 Ellitson was the local butcher. Photographs taken during the siege show a tree from which cattle, and later horses, were hung up after slaughter. Judging from the background of these photographs, this tree was sited somewhere on the fringe of the stadt. It is safe to adduce, therefore, that this was the slaughter pole which Ellitson erected, and to which Plaatje refers here.

4 Dutch: literally, 'red-neck'. This was a nickname given to the British by the Boers. It derives from the fact that when light-skinned Englishmen first came into contact with the South African sun their skins tended to redden from sunburn. The unprotected neck is particularly sensitive to this, and invariably the men concerned found themselves sporting red napes.

5 Dutch: 'damned' or 'blasted'.

6 Sotho-Tswana: 'become fat'. The implication is that horse meal was mixed into the grain to fatten it, thus providing a more substantial meal.

7 There was no fort named White. Perhaps this refers to the women's laager, as the passage immediately following suggests. It is possible that he intended 'Whiteley's fort' – for the Mayor spent much of his time organizing and supervising the women's laager. That this error of partial omission is likely, we may adduce from the fact that this passage is again in the second handwriting. As before, it is far more careless and primitive than the rest of the text.

8 Tswana: 'to poke at the wasps'. (This is similar to the English phrase 'disturb a hornet's nest'.)

9 The question of Britain's preparedness for war is an interesting and perhaps controversial one. There are many pre-war reports of statesmen, both in England and in Cape Town, denying its possibility and arguing that overt preparation might mean precipitation. We know that Baden-Powell's efforts to equip and train a force had to be done with the utmost discretion. This is why the argument that the Commanding Officer in Mafeking organized the siege to commit Boer troops and thus buy time for Britain cannot be dismissed, but it implied committing 1 200 whites and nearly 10 000 Barolong to the trials of war. Hence it is easy to understand Plaatje's lamentations and recriminations.

10 Maritzani (more commonly spelt Mareetsane) is a village of the Barolong boo Ratshidi and fell under the jurisdiction of their chief. It is situated about 25 miles south-south-west of Mafeking.

11 Plaatje seems to have had an insatiable appetite for eliciting news. He was, during the siege, often sick in body and frustrated in mind. But if anything made him feel better it was – as on this occasion – the arrival of information from outside. The juxtaposition here of his statement about his own feelings and the news itself is slightly confusing as he makes no introductory remarks to precede the latter.

12 As Mareetsane fell within the borders of the Cape Colony, allegiance to the Boers was regarded as an act of rebellion against Britain.

13 Hard Labour.

14 Alfred Ngidi was a railwayman, of Mfengu origin. It was not the first time Ngidi and Plaatje had encountered one another in court. In June 1899 Plaatje had sued Ngidi after a dispute over the hiring of Plaatje's musical organ, and successfully recovered the sum of 7s 6d.

15 Dutch: literally, 'a brick (loaf) of bread'.

16 It is interesting to read one of the reminders printed in the *Mafeking Mail* on the subject. Dated 2 January, it states the following:

Merchants, Traders, Shopkeepers, etc. are prohibited from selling Mealies, Mealie Meal, Kaffir Corn or Grain of any sort. There are three Grain Stores existing at which purchase of Grain may be made, viz.:

No. 1. Native Stadt.
No. 2. Native Location.
No. 3. Lippmann's Yard, Town Store (For Townspeople).
It has come to notice that several people who have small quantities of Mealie Meal and Grain in thier possession are in the habit of handing over to their servants certain bulk quantities in order that the servants may feed themselves. This causes unnecessary waste. Servants should be put on rations by their masters daily. The following quantities should amply suffice under present circumstances:
1 lb. to 1½ lbs. of Mealie Meal or Grain, proportionate deduction being made when Native women or children have to be fed, such as ½ to ¾ lb. per diem.

C. M. RYAN, Capt.
Mafeking 30th Dec., 1899.   D.A.A.G.

17 Another commodity is mentioned, but as it is indecipherable in the text it has been omitted.
18 'Our' here appears to refer to the Barolong and location-dwellers. 'Common person' immediately before probably refers strictly to the whites.
19 The last two sentences (again, it seems, dictated by the diarist to some other scribe) are incoherently phrased. They have been changed around so as to render them comprehensible.
20 Serolong is the language of the Barolong. (It is also used indigenously to mean the culture of the Barolong.) In English conversation 'Serolong' and 'Barolong' are often confused, for their contextual referents are not perfectly translatable.
21 Sotho-Tswana: 'Barolong women'. -ali (pronounced -adi) is the Sotho-Tswana feminine suffix.
22 i.e., the three grain-stores. Brewing beer was, traditionally, women's work.
23 i.e., collected.
24 It appears that this is Plaatje's own label for the protest by the Barolong women.
25 Xhosa-Zulu: 'recommend', 'praise', 'commend', 'extol'. (The c here is a dental click.) The implication is that this was specially remarked upon.
26 Mafeking (properly Mafikeng) was the daughter of Molema, founder of Mafikeng. She was married to Lekoko (see entry for 29 December). It was with her brother Silas Molema's family that Plaatje lived during the siege.
27 Tswana: 'a sudden piercing pain in the chest; angina pectoris' (J. Tom Brown, Secwana–English Dictionary, 1931.)
28 This is merely Plaatje's way of saying, with a modicum of tact, that Selabi's story was fabricated. As there is no mention that Selabi was a despatch runner, it is possible that he was a diviner.
29 From here this entry is written in pencil shorthand. The script is very faint, but part of the text is written in long hand on the previous page, so that an almost complete translation was possible. (The two entries have been amalgamated to produce the fullest possible version.) Expert opinion has suggested that, judging from the script itself, Plaatje had just learnt the art – but that he was a talented student. There are two possible reasons for this particular entry being written in shorthand: either, as a legally minded citizen, he did not want the reader to know that he was accused of thieving (for that part of the text is not reproduced in long hand), or he simply wanted to practise the art.
30 Dutch: 'boss', 'master'. Plaatje would seem to be referring here to Bell.
31 There are a few faint words after this, but they have proved too faint to decipher.
32 'Patrick' is Patrick Sidzumo, court messenger in Mafeking from July 1899 to July 1901. He also served as a corporal in the 'Fingo Continent' during the siege.

33 This shorthand passage ends here. In a few instances the quotation marks are omitted in the text. They have been inserted.

34 Bell may have meant 'your father's generation'. Plaatje's father did live in the Mafeking district in the 1890's, but died in 1896, before Bell arrived to take up the position of Resident Magistrate and Civil Commissioner. There is no evidence to suggest that Bell and Plaatje's father had ever met.

35 George Mfazi was the leader of the ill-fated Mfengu raiding party ambushed by the Boers in April. The Lumatas concerned were probably Lucas and Mark Lumata, both leading members of the Mfengu community in Mafeking.

36 He means 'accidents' or 'setbacks'. The week had, it is true, been unfortunate for the beleaguered. For example: on the first of January a carpenter, Slater, was killed; on the second, a niece of the chief and several others were killed in the stadt; on the third, two children were killed in the women's laager; on the fourth, typhoid broke out in the women's laager.

37 The fact that the defending troops were constantly being redeployed gave Barolong youths an opportunity to earn small sums as porters.

38 i.e., the chief gunner.

39 Tswana: 'I knew that he directed them to the town backyard which was there.' The Tswana spelling is interspersed with Sotho orthographic usage. *Sekgotlho* is usually used to describe the rear section of a homestead; hence we translate it as 'backyard'. In fact, the sentence is curiously written; rather than *toropo e sekgotlho*, it should have been *segotlho ea toropo*. Perhaps this reflects the fact that it is a child speaking. Plaatje's young informant was trying to explain that the gunner was the only one who could effectively aim the gun on the town.

40 Sotho-Tswana: 'gentle rain, long continued' (Brown, *Secwana–English Dictionary*, 1931).

41 From this and a previous entry we learn that members of the (ethnically mixed) Black Watch had a habit of apprehending returning cattle-raiders in an attempt to dispossess them of their loot. The authorities were worried about this as a threat to law and order; but Plaatje was concerned for a more fundamental economic reason – the discouraging of suppliers.

42 Sotho-Tswana: *kgotla* has a wide range of meaning. The usual primary translation given is 'council-place' (Brown, *Secwana–English Dictionary*; T. J. Kriel, *New English–Sesotho Dictionary*, 1958). However, in some places *kgotla* is also used to describe political units of various orders, such as wards and sections. (See Schapera, *The Tswana*, 1953.) *Kgotla* also refers to the meeting-enclosure that is usually found in each ward. *Lekgotla* is a 'council', but modern Tshidi tend to drop the prefix *le-*. There is a degree of local variation in the range of meaning that the word covers. Here *kgotlas* (the English plural suffix *-s* replacing the Sotho-Tswana class-five [plural] prefix *ma-*) refers to 'wards'. (For a discussion of these political units, see Schapera, *Handbook of Tswana Law and Custom*, 1938.)

43 'Mathlaseloa' refers to the age-regiment formed in 1887 under Badirile Mont-shiwa's leadership. 'Lethlaseloakazi' refers to the female equivalent.

44 i.e., the beer.

45 He refers here to the rinderpest epidemic of 1896 which reduced Barolong herds drastically. It was a historical event recalled long afterwards and used to date the people and occurrences of the era.

46 *Mafeking Mail*, 13 January; by this time the situation in the stadt was beginning to look very serious and rationing was much tighter than in town. Many of the poverty-stricken survived on the horse-meat soup made by five kitchens: three in the stadt, one in the location and one in the town. A foul-smelling horse-meat factory was set up south-west of the town. This began to produce everything from brawn and sausages to stuffing for pillows. The popularity of this food rose in correspondence with the decrease in the availability of alternatives.

47 Madikwe is the original Setswana name for the Marico district of the Western Transvaal. It is also the name of a Bahurutshe boo Mokgatlha village about thirty miles north-east of Zeerust.
48 McMullen's Farm was about two-and-a-half miles east of town.
49 Dutch: 'watch out' or 'take care'.
50 The *Mafeking Mail* did not publish an edition until the 21st as a result.
51 Sotho-Tswana: 'a head of cattle with (literally, "of") lung sickness'.
52 A perimeter defensive fort to the west of town.
53 Dutch: 'strong'.
54 Sotho-Tswana: 'Yes . . . I understand (hear) . . . I understand well . . . the way he speaks . . . I say, Sir . . . he says . . .'
55 From here until the end of the month the entries are in shorthand. One reason for this passage being written may have been the pressure of time.
56 This was repeated in the proclamation issued by Baden-Powell on the 21st (which Plaatje mentions in the next entry). The extent of the rationing was announced by Captain Ryan on the same day: 'Full ration, European: Men 2/–, women, half ration, 1s, children under 14, 6d.' This statement is not entirely clear, for we are not quite sure whether this meant that the stated amount could be spent on every occasion that an individual went (by arrangement) to a store. At this time Barolong men (full ration) were permitted to spend 6d.
57 The shops which were permitted to retail foodstuffs under supervision of the authorities.
58 That this is not clear is a result of the fact that the rationing arrangements were still confused. People were, at the time, in the process of registering and receiving ration tickets, and supply-scales had been announced, but the mechanics of distribution were yet to be clarified.
59 The first two paragraphs of the proclamation read as follows: 'I hereby proclaim and direct that on and after the 21st instant all shops will close for the sale of foodstuffs in any form. Stock lists to be sent in to Capt. Ryan, D.A.A.G., of all supplies then on hand and these will be held as strictly in bond for the Imperial Authorities.' (*Mafeking Mail*, 21 January.)
60 See note 26 above.
61 'Raseleji' (Ra-Seleje) is Silas Molema, father of Seleje.
62 It has proved impossible to obtain any information about this person.
63 'Ntsala Sakaria' (translated, Cousin Sakaria) is Zacharia Schiemann, Ebie's brother and the diarist's cousin. He was 26 years of age at the time of his death.
64 The entry is unfinished. The alarm that he mentions must have been false, for had the Sunday truce been violated it would have been recorded by one or another of the sources.

CHAPTER 4

FEBRUARY 1900

1 The diarist's stallion. Plaatje took a keen interest in horses and continually expressed the fear (later realized) that hunger would force the general population of Mafeking to eat horseflesh.
2 Or Basotho. Oral tradition has it that this group of Basotho migrated to the Mafeking District in the time of Montshiwa I (1849–96). They were allotted land on the fringe of the stadt.

3 Pitsane, now a Barolong boo Ratlou village, lies approximately forty miles west-north-west of Mafeking, on the Molopo river. It should not be confused with Pitsane (formerly spelt Pitsani) in Botswana, from which the Jameson Raid was mounted. Plaatje's figure (48) may represent the mileage of the route taken.

4 Situated 38 miles south-east of Mafeking.

5 The paragraph was subject to much overwritten addition, all of which has been included here.

6 The Boers were well aware of the vital contribution made by Barolong cattle-raiders to the waning food-stocks in Mafeking. Further, the herds so frequently raided were an important source of sustenance for the besiegers themselves. Consequently, they attempted to place them as far behind their own lines as logistics permitted.

7 Dutch: 'cattle-byre'.

8 Tswana: literally, 'Get out! Get out! They [the cattle] belong to [are of] Morolong [i.e., the Barolong chief]. Now they do not belong to the Boers!' These words were shouted by the raiders at the herders [presumably Rapulana-Barolong employed by the Boers]. The word *ele* in the final sentence is slightly puzzling; it implies a relative construction [literal translation: 'Now they [the cattle] do not belong, they [the cattle] of the Boers']. Liberty to translate the sentence more freely has been taken.

9 Xhosa: 'the self', 'personality', 'individuality', 'body', 'substance'. Zulu: 'root', 'basis', 'charm against evil', 'badge of bravery'. Plaatje probably chose this word to convey a wide range of meaning clustering around the notion of individuality/personality.

10 That this was not usually the case, even as regards these risky raids, is amply illustrated in the diary. Plaatje appears to have been put into a pessimistic mood by the coincidence of unfortunate occurrences.

11 A corruption of the Dutch *pelsjas* – 'fur skin jacket', which article was believed, if specially made for the purpose by an African ritual expert, to protect the wearer from harm. It is possible that Plaatje, an ardent Christian, is using the Dutch to emphasize the humour of the situation: Boers, a profoundly religious population, obtain charmed skin-jackets (from 'natives' who are characterized by them as being superstitious non-Christians) for magical protection which are then thought to help the *wearers* in a confrontation with Barolong.

12 Field-cornet.

13 M.D. here refers not to a Western medical doctor but a traditional priest-doctor. The Tswana term for the latter – *ngaka* – has been extended, since contact, to mean the former as well, so that there is no linguistic differentiation between the two. Plaatje introduces this into English by using M.D. to refer to a priest-doctor. This is a continuation of the *peljase* incident; the humour of the inversion is patent, especially in the light of the rest of the sentence.

14 Dutch: 'bone out of the foot of an ox or a horse'; more specifically a 'witch-doctor's divination-bone' (in Sotho-Tswana *ditaola*). Traditionally, knowledge of their use was a carefully protected secret.

15 Plaatje, besides working as interpreter and clerk for the Civil Commissioner, acted also as unofficial administrator of the latter's organization of African welfare during the siege.

16 This figure is probably reasonably accurate. Plaatje was involved in organizing a stadt census, completed on 22 March 1900, which registered 5 448 inhabitants. Plaatje then calculated that half the population of the stadt must have left since the commencement of the siege: the African population was being encouraged to leave and seek refuge with allies elsewhere as supplies were on the wane. The first mention of an organized exodus was on 27 February, so that at this time, with emigration occurring in a haphazard manner, the figure of 7 000 is quite probable.

17 This was a stronghold to the north-west of Godley's western headquarters, its summit dominating his advanced positions. It was armed with a seven-pounder.

18 Moathloli Mokoto, a close friend and contemporary of the diarist, and a farmer by occupation.

19 The name of his horse.

20 Plaatje persistently uses the phrase 'narrow escapade' instead of 'narrow escape'.

21 'At Crocodile Pools Colonel Plumer is opposed by the Boers entrenched in a strong position; our force is equally strongly posted, and has already caused the enemy serious losses with its shell fire. More men and guns are come to reinforce it, and it will then proceed to run the Boers out.' (*Mafeking Mail*, 8 February 1900.)

22 'From 7th inst. inclusive all employees of Native Labour will be required to take out a Pass for each Native employed by them. The Passes can be obtained between the hours of 10.30 a.m. and 1 p.m. at the Resident Magistrate's Office, and that official will keep a Register of all those issued. Passes will be shown when required by military or civil authorities and any Native found in the town without a Pass will be liable to be punished by the Court of Summary Jurisdiction.' (*Mafeking Mail*, 6 February 1900.)

   '. . . the term Native Servants applies to all Natives in the employ of persons living in the town . . . the term Native applies to Bechuanas, Matabeles, and all those belonging to original tribes of this country . . . Natives belonging to enrolled Native Contingents, who may desire to visit the town, should obtain a Pass from the Office commanding the Corps . . . Native labourers in the employ of the Government will be engaged in the Stadt by one of the Overseers . . . The men will be brought up to the town in charge of the Overseer, who will be held responsible for seeing that the men leave the town as soon as they are paid.'   Signed E. H. Cecil, Major, Chief Staff Officer. (*Mafeking Mail*, 8 February 1900)

23 All attempts to trace this document in archives have failed.

24 This paragraph is written in shorthand in the diary, and there is evidence that its use here is the result of the diarist being in considerable haste. (There are numerous corrections and deletions.)

25 Existing supplies of conventional foodstuffs were calculated to last in the stadt until the end of March. Horses were indeed eaten thereafter, though we will never know of what Plaatje's diet consisted after his last diary entry.

26 'Ganankoto' is Ganankoto Thomas Monyapeng (or Thomas Ganankoto Monyapeng). He was Silas Molema's carriage-driver after the siege and may have been engaged by Bell in a similar capacity during the siege. 'Ganankoto' means 'a man with no legs', thus Plaatje's word-play.

27 Dutch: 'Gentle Annie' was a five-pounder Krupp.

28 Probably Gabriel Andrew (or Andreas) Plaatje, an elder brother of the diarist. He and his family lived at Mayakgoro, an outstation of the Berlin Mission Society in the Phokwane district.

29 Plaatje's wife and son had been in Burghersdorp (Cape Colony) at the outbreak of war, but may subsequently have visited relatives at Bethanie in the Orange Free State. This would explain Plaatje's reference to 'Free State'.

30 i.e., the runners.

31 Tswana: 'jump to', 'jump into' (Sotho: 'jump to', 'exaggerate'). This verb is written in the applicative form.

32 A popular Barolong siege-hero, this man was a cattle-raider whose boldness and bravery were recalled for many years afterwards.

33 Bathoen I, chief of the Bangwaketse at Kanye.

34 Mr James Dall, Mafeking town councillor, died on this day.

35 Gopane (formerly Gopanestadt) is a village of the Bahurutshe ba ga Gopane and lies forty miles north-north-east of Mafeking. It is also sometimes referred to as Manoane or Maanwane.

36 Dutch: 'bad', 'poor'.

37 Dutch: 'council'.

38 Ernest Grayson, a graduate of Cambridge University, joined the staff of the office of the Magistrate and Civil Commissioner in Mafeking as second clerk in 1898, shortly before Plaatje. During the siege Grayson joined the Town Guard, and Plaatje took over many of his usual duties.

39 This sentence is incomplete in the diary.

40 This refers to the annexation of British Bechuanaland to the Cape Colony, in 1895.

41 i.e., charged.

42 i.e., highly inflammable.

43 Probably a piece of phosphorus, used in incendiaries at the time.

44 i.e., those brought in by Mathakgong on the eleventh.

45 This is a surprising statement, as meat in Mafeking was now scarce. There is no other reference to the incident, although thanks are offered to Mathakgong in the *Mafeking Mail* of 16 February, for the 'succulent, juicy, undercut' that appeared on 'certain breakfast tables'. This article was in fact written by Plaatje (originally as a report to Mr Bell), and is reproduced in full in the plate section.

46 Written in margin: 'The Big [Gun] round to the west now. It sent several shells into the stadt. One burst onto one of the Wessels' houses. Killed one woman and wounded 3. The gun going to the far end of the garrison is a clear proof that the Boers are masters of the situation.'

47 By this time Elizabeth and St Leger were probably back in Burghersdorp, staying with Leah M'belle, Elizabeth's mother.

48 A girl of fourteen years, she was the daughter of Lekoko and Mafikeng. Emang served as a young housekeeper for Plaatje for a period during the siege.

49 See the entry of 30 December.

50 'Malibali' is Malibali Matilda Dira, a niece to Mafikeng and cousin to Emang. She later married Thomas Maseng.

51 'Masiako' is Baetlhoi, wife of Molema Tawana. Her eldest son was Israel Mosiako Molema.

52 Mamoathloli was presumably Mrs Mokoto. Morara Molema remembered her as 'an old woman who brought up (his eldest sister) Seleje'.

53 This entry is in shorthand and gives evidence of much haste, although it is clear and decipherable.

54 This refers to Friday, 16 February.

55 This entry is written in shorthand.

56 Tributary of the Orange River with its source in the Orange Free State. At the time, this was the British 'front'.

57 Sotho-Tswana: 'When it is not for a person to cry out [call], God calls.' The comma is an editorial insertion. This may be interpreted in one of two ways. Either Plaatje is saying that when a person is powerless God comes to his aid (which makes sense in terms of the sentences that come before and after); or he is suggesting a Job-like resignation to God's actions.

58 In the margin alongside this entry is written: 'One of the runners was wounded when they were crossing the enemy's lines from the south this morning.'

59 The entries for 21 and 22 February are written in shorthand.

60 Joshua Molema, brother of Silas T. Molema.

61 See entry for Saturday, 10 February.

62 Food was, by this time, the major preoccupation of all. Compare Plaatje's remarks with the entry in the diary of Major F. D. Baillie (*Mafeking*) for

19 February: 'We went out to try and shoot plover, which form an acceptable addition to our rations, as we have now come down to horse-flesh and six ounces of bread per day.'

63 Malmani (Molemane or Ottoshoop) lies about twenty miles north-east of Mafeking, along the road to Zeerust.

64 Sergeant-Major Looney was accused of selling government supplies.

65 The diarist wrote 'Looney', obviously in error. The text has been corrected here.

66 By 'securities' Plaatje presumably meant (military) security guards.

67 Probably: 'like Mamasinobe's (son) Ralisa'.

68 Dutch: 'the esquire Bell', although clumsy, is perhaps the closest possible translation.

69 The *Mafeking Mail* of 17 February refers to Snyman's letters as having arrived 'a few days ago'.

70 Kimberley had actually been relieved on 15 February; but Ladysmith was not to be relieved until 28 February. News of this did not reach Mafeking until early March.

71 *Mafeking Mail*, 25 February: 'Lord Roberts has arrived in South Africa with Lord Kitchener as his Chief Staff Officer, and reinforcements are daily arriving.'

72 In the margin across this and the following entry Plaatje has written: 'I don't think I have mentioned that the Lothlakane people took up arms against us.'

73 i.e., in terms of the strategy mentioned in the entry for 10 February, Africans were encouraged to leave Mafeking for Kanye, in an attempt to make food-resources go as far as possible. Plaatje was instrumental in organizing this.

74 Saane was headman of the village of Molimola. He distinguished himself in the early months of the siege by assisting Mafeking's runners and cattle-raiders from the outside. Later he was captured by the Boers and removed to Lotlhakane, from where he provided the garrison with invaluable intelligence reports through a network of runners. The British regarded his capture, somewhat paradoxically, as an infringement of the agreement on 'native' neutrality, informally entered into at the start of the siege. (See S. T. Plaatje, *Native Life in South Africa*, p. 243.)

75 Genealogically the most senior of the Tswana tribes, the Hurutshe were often thought of by Barolong as an unduly passive people.

76 Colonel Plumer's regiment initially took up a position at Tuli (on the Limpopo) to defend Rhodesia. He had commenced moving southwards, however, and was at this time occupying both Kanye and Crocodile Pools.

77 John Tengo Jabavu was a well-known African politician, and editor of the influential African weekly newspaper, *Imvo Zabantsundu*. Over the next few years Plaatje and Jabavu were to come to know one another well, and Jabavu became godfather to Plaatje's daughter Olive, born in 1903. Later, Plaatje and Jabavu came into conflict over Jabavu's support for the Natives' Land Act of 1913.

78 Cape Police.

79 Situated north-west of the town, *en route* to Kanye.

80 An interesting title, considering subsequent South African history.

81 Sing., *lekatane*. Tswana: 'Kaffir melons', 'vegetable marrows' (Brown, *Secwana–English Dictionary*, 1931). Sotho: 'large species of bitter melon', 'Kaffir melons' (Kriel, *New English–Sesotho Dictionary*, 1958). Among Barolong it refers only to melons, not marrows.

82 The words 'were lamb, veal, and no horse flesh' were written in shorthand.

83 Presumably the area of the Shangaan encampment.

84 Dutch: 'nothing'.

85 It is impossible to be sure who this was. Morara Molema believed he may have been Taolo Sekgoro.

86 Maphachwe is the name of a depression north-west of the stadt. It lies immediately behind Seoding, Plaatje's home.
87 This and the following entry are in shorthand.
88 This is the first allusion to the matter in the diary. Bell's own diary does not mention the matter.

CHAPTER 5

MARCH 1900

1 Plaatje began work in the Kimberley Post Office seven years before. 'Service' refers to the Cape Civil Service.
2 From here to the end of the day's entry the text is in shorthand.
3 From here to the end of the day's entry the text is in shorthand.
4 Sergeant-Major William Ashton Taylor, of the Colonial Contingent.
5 Johannes Jongilanga Sidzumo, a local farmer and father of Patrick, the court messenger. Johannes Sidzumo and his family had trekked from the Transkei (Tsolo district) in the early 1890s and later settled at Moleloane, a few miles north-west of Mafeking. The family moved within the town's perimeter at the outbreak of war.
6 From here until the end of the day's entry shorthand has been used. This switch from longhand to shorthand, soon after the start of an entry, seems to have been occasioned by haste.
7 Cape Police.
8 See 27 February. In that context it is spelt 'Maphachwe'.
9 Tswana (properly *moretlhwa*): 'a bush bearing edible brown berries' (Sotho: 'the plant *Grewia occidentalis* or four corners, *kruisbessie*'. See T. J. Kriel, *New English–Sesotho Dictionary*, 1958). Phrased thus, it is intended to indicate that the boy had been eating the berries.
10 i.e., the boy that Plaatje met.
11 A town on the Modder River, ner Kimberley, but in the Orange Free State.
12 The entries for the next two days are written in shorthand.
13 i.e., 'Cape Boys', the coloured contingent then under the command of Sergeant Currie. Literally, the appellation means 'Cape people' (Dutch).
14 On 1 March the *Mafeking Mail* noted: 'A letter has been sent to General Snyman by the Colonel Commanding to the following effect: "That as General Snyman has used armed Natives for the invasion of our territory, and is employing them directly against us, the Colonel proposed to act in a similar manner." Snyman probably wished intelligence to filter back to Mafeking to the effect that these men had now been disarmed – implying that the O.C. should follow suit. Information implanted in this manner stood a far greater chance of being believed than did an official letter.
15 A rumour had circulated that the Boers were preparing to leave and had placed a dummy in 'Sanna's' position as a ruse. The fact that the barrel was, on several occasions, elevated without the gun being fired added to the widespread conviction. The rumour was dispelled the following day.
16 Ben Weil.
17 See notes to the entry for Tuesday, 27 February.
18 This epigrammatic format was used by the *Mafeking Mail* ('Special Edition' of 8 March) to herald this news.
19 The English press at the time consistently referred to the Boers as 'women slayers'. Incidents in which women and children, both within and outside the

laagers, had allegedly been fired upon by the enemy were seized upon to substantiate this view.

20 i.e., his generalship is at an end.

21 The Barolong boo Rapulana, at Lotlhakane (Rietfontein).

22 Lobatse lies 47 miles north of Mafeking in Botswana (then the Bechuanaland Protectorate).

23 Signal Hill is situated three miles north-north-east of Mafeking.

24 There is no previous mention of them.

25 Madibe Siding is approximately ten miles to the south-west of Mafeking and lay in Tshidi-Barolong territory.

26 '"old Barwise"' is William Barwise of the farm Nottingham, which lay in the vicinity of Rooidammetjies.

27 Tswana: 'Restrain them [the cattle], let us fight for them [the cattle]. They laugh and say, We are young boys of writing who are not able to defend ourselves. These Boers, even the English, are accustomed to hand over everything of ours. They want them [the cattle] standing [and] us to fight for them.' The meaning of the first sentence is clear. By the second, Mathakgong means that the Boers laugh at them, saying that because they are literate (Barolong, among tribes in the area, being thought of as having a high level of literacy and of being inept in battle), they are weak. He continues to imply that the English were used to conceding Barolong interests in the face of Boer demands – a view that was gaining support among some Barolong at the time.

28 i.e., on the raid. 'Teacher' Potiphar was Potiphar Moshoela, believed to have taught at the Wesleyan mission school in the stadt.

29 See the entry for 6 November.

30 Captain Marsh (Royal West Kent Regiment) commanded a squadron of the Protectorate Regiment.

31 A village five miles north-west of Mafeking.

32 See note 1 to entry of 25 February.

33 Only one siege survivor in the early 1970s could recall these names, and could provide no more information than that they were foreigners who lived in the location.

34 Or Bodibe, about twenty miles south-east of Mafeking.

35 Dutch: 'Here are the Kaffirs.'

36 Civil Commissioner and Resident Magistrate (C. G. H. Bell).

37 Sotho: 'We are frightened by roaring only.' Presumably Plaatje intends that they had overestimated Boer strength in that area; it was their 'roaring' (perhaps gunfire) that gave the impression they were numerous.

38 This refers to the Rapulana-Barolong who were Boer allies.

39 In the stadt.

40 Notice of this order was first served by Lord E. H. Cecil in the *Mafeking Mail*, 19 February 1900.

41 *Titshalakazi* (Xhosa: a female teacher) refers to Miss S. J. Ngono of the stadt Wesleyan Mission School. Her fiancé ('Gun'), a member of the 'Black Watch', had died of wounds sustained in action during January. See the entry for 7 January.

42 See entry for 10 February 1900.

43 A friend of Plaatje's, living near Setlagoli. The name should be contracted into one word and not written as two.

44 This Barolong boo Ratlou village lay approximately 48 miles south-west of Mafeking.

45 The 'Big Hole' of Kimberley.

46 Sotho-Tswana (in combination): 'They will hate one another.' This sentence is puzzling in this context for, despite the punctuation, it is not clear how it relates to the preceding lines. Perhaps it is intended to refer to the Boer prisoners and their captors.

47 Tswana: literally, 'Die having conquered for yourself.' *Ikaletse* (past applicative) here should be spelt *ikhaletse*; this omission could be a function of the
orthographic confusion of that era.

48 The mission station and diamond-digging centre near Barkly West, Cape
Province, where Plaatje grew up and received much of his education.

49 Abel Pienaar was a man of Griqua origin, a resident of the Pniel mission
station and assistant to the missionary in charge, Rev. Ernst Westphal. Simon
Plaatje, Plaatje's eldest brother, and his mother, as well as other members of
his family, were still living at Pniel, so his concern at what had been
happening there was understandable.

50 i.e., Barkly West.

51 Rev. Ernst Westphal, Plaatje's former teacher at Pniel, and a naturalized
British subject, was arrested by the British military authorities on the grounds
that he had, between November 1899 and February 1900, aided Boer forces
after their occupation of the Pniel district. Although much of the evidence
against Westphal was of a somewhat dubious nature, he was eventually
brought to trial in 1903 and convicted of high treason (second class), and
disfranchised for five years. The main charge on which he was found guilty
was that he had assisted Boer forces in the construction of a telegraph line
across the Pniel estate.

52 Henry Burton, South African politician and statesman, was admitted to the
bar in 1892 and thereafter practised in Kimberley. After the Jameson Raid
in 1895 he became a strong supporter of the Afrikander Bond, and, in the
general election in 1898, unsuccessfully contested the Barkly West constituency
(which included the Pniel mission) against Cecil Rhodes. He was eventually
elected to Parliament for another Cape constituency in 1902. He later became
Attorney-General and, after the Union of South Africa in 1909, held the
ministries of Native Affairs, Railways and Finance at different times. For a
number of years Plaatje was to enjoy a close relationship with him.

53 Plaatje often referred later in life to the case of *Rex v. Mankazana* in June 1898,
in which Burton accepted a brief from the African community and won an
important legal victory which limited the operation of the pass laws in
Kimberley.

54 i.e., the relief troops.

55 Dutch: 'shelter'.

56 Margin note here reads: 'Heard in the Court of Summary Jurisdiction on
Monday, March 19th, before His Hon., Maj. H. J. Goold-Adams and Lt.-Col.
Hore.'

57 i.e., Shangaan.

58 i.e., Bechuanalander.

59 Bechuanaland Protectorate.

60 Dutch: 'thin', 'emaciated'.

61 An outer area of the stadt.

62 A railway cottage five miles from Mafeking on the line to the south known as
Five Mile Cottage.

63 Sotho-Tswana: correctly, *ngwan'a molimo* (a contraction of *ngwana a molimo*), it
means (literally) 'child of god' or 'young god'. The English '*s* is obviously
meant to replace the Sotho-Tswana possessive, despite the fact that it is
written in the wrong place.

64 Dutch: 'shepherd'.

65 Sotho: 'guide'. (The Tswana equivalent is *moshupiwatsela*.) 'Keshupile' is
Keshupile Tlatsana. He was mentioned in General Orders, 24 May, for his
gallantry during the Boer attack of 12 May.

66 Tshipithata Motshegare, a younger brother of Josiah Motshegare (see note
70 below).

67 Sotho-Tswana: 'ruins'.
68 Macheng Pan lies to the east of a Barolong farm, Oxpan, in Botswana. It is (as the crow flies) 28 miles north-west of Mafeking.
69 This is a Batlharo village twenty miles north-west of Mafeking.
70 Although there is a full stop after the word, it appears that Plaatje had intended to continue. Tshipithata is the name of a man mentioned both before and after this entry.
71 Rev. Davidson Msikinya was the Wesleyan minister, and member of a prominent family, who officiated at Plaatje's marriage to Elizabeth in Kimberley in 1898.
72 On this day there were more shells fired at Mafeking than on any other during the siege.
73 i.e., the Court of Summary Jurisdiction.
74 *Mafeking Mail*, 27 March: 'Corroboration has been received from several sources that relief, from the south, is now well this side of Vryburg.'
75 In fact, they did read it that day.
76 i.e., for not having told his brother-in-law, Isaiah Bud-M'belle.
77 Probably a man called Rajane Nkgoang.
78 Xhosa: 'This man wants to buy a horse at £15, but he is waiting for me to arrive.'
79 Xhosa: 'Therefore he went with it [i.e., the horse] to town and I never did see it.' *Edolopene* is wrongly spelt; it shoud read *edolophini*.
80 Probably a reference to Joseph Singapi Moss, a court interpreter and a prominent member of Kimberley's African community, whom Plaatje knew well. 'Dingiswayo *vs* Moss' was probably a case heard in the Kimberley Magistrate's Court or the Griqualand West High Court, but it has not been possible to trace it.
81 i.e., Rajane. See note 78 above.
82 'Teacher's fort' possibly refers to the Mathlaseloa redoubt ('Badirile's Fort'), which Teacher Kolobe Dinku commanded.
83 Baden-Powell.
84 Despatch rider.
85 Tswana: 'A species of vegetable with a spinach flavour.'
86 This style of expression is a result of direct translation from Setswana. It is frequently heard among present-day Barolong.
87 As this letter is an important indicator of the situation at the time when Plaatje chose to discontinue his entries, it has been decided to reproduce it in full (*Mafeking Mail*, 29 March). After this last entry there is a copy of a letter obviously written some time before. Because its content is not relevant to the diary itself, it has been omitted.
88 Grinnell-Milne, *Baden-Powell at Mafeking*, p. 179.

Index of names